WITHDRAWN
NDSU

EDUCATIONAL ASSESSMENT

EDUCATIONAL ASSESSMENT

Insuring That All Students Succeed in School

By

ALBERT H. BRIGANCE

*Adjunct Professor
Department of Educational and
Counseling Psychology
The University of Tennessee
Knoxville, Tennessee*

and

CHARLES H. HARGIS

*Professor
Department of Special Services Education
The University of Tennessee
Knoxville, Tennessee*

CHARLES C THOMAS • PUBLISHER
Springfield • Illinois • U.S.A.

Published and Distributed Throughout the World by
CHARLES C THOMAS • PUBLISHER
2600 South First Street
Springfield, Illinois 62794-9265

This book is protected by copyright. No part of
it may be reproduced in any manner without
written permission from the publisher.

© *1993 by* CHARLES C THOMAS • PUBLISHER
ISBN 0-398-05884-0
Library of Congress Catalog Card Number: 93-11512

With THOMAS BOOKS *careful attention is given to all details of manufacturing and design. It is the Publisher's desire to present books that are satisfactory as to their physical qualities and artistic possibilities and appropriate for their particular use.* THOMAS BOOKS *will be true to those laws of quality that assure a good name and good will.*

Printed in the United States of America
SC-R-3

Library of Congress Cataloging-in-Publication Data

Brigance, Albert H. (Albert Henry), 1932–
    Educational assessment : insuring that all students succeed in school / by Albert H. Brigance and Charles H. Hargis.
      p.   cm.
    Includes bibliographical references (p.) and index.
    ISBN 0-398-05883-0
    1. Educational tests and measurements—United States.
2. Students—United States—Rating of.   I. Hargis, Charles H.
II. Title.
LB3051.B696   1993
371.2'6'0973—dc20   93-11512
                                                                        CIP

PREFACE

The writing of this book was prompted by needs we felt were unmet by current texts on educational assessment. Some needs are those of the many students who are not being served well in our schools. These are the students who are failing to progress, most of whom ultimately drop out. Other needs are related but are those of the teachers who must deal with the problem of the students that are casualties of the inadequacies of our current assessment systems.

Another need is to fill a shortcoming in our educational philosophy. This shortcoming has to do with our definition of success, or lack thereof. Generally, we all seem cognizant of the importance of success in educational achievement. However, we have been unable to define it in terms that permit it to be measured and then to consciously produce through educational intervention. We attempt to do these things in this book.

This book is not another anthology of tests and assessment techniques. We focus on the issue of success and its maintenance. We believe the instrument for attaining success is to be found in the methods of assessment. These methods are very much in the hands of teachers. Also, the methods are relatively simple and very much related to curriculum and instructional activity.

In short, our purpose for the book is to insure that students succeed in school. No student should be failing in our educational system. Success is productive. Failure of the chronic sort many of our students experience is worse than nonproductive; its consequences are devastating.

A.H.B.
C.H.H.

CONTENTS

		Page
Preface		v
Chapter		
1.	Assessment and Curriculum—What's the Relationship?	3
2.	Success and Failure	24
3.	Types of Tests	45
4.	Reliability and Validity	64
5.	Tests for Instruction: Success-Based Assessment	81
6.	The Best Assessor for Planning Instruction—The Teacher	93
7.	Effective Curriculum-Based Assessment	105
8.	Tests for Accountability	123
9.	Grading	131
10.	Success-Based Assessment and School Organization	141
11.	Vision and Hearing	160
	References	169
	Index	171

EDUCATIONAL ASSESSMENT

Chapter 1

ASSESSMENT AND CURRICULUM— WHAT'S THE RELATIONSHIP?

Does the adoption of a test lead to the development of a curriculum or does the adoption of a curriculum lead to the development of a test? Actually, either is a likely possibility. The national debate that concerns achievement testing has led to the recognition that the development of such tests will naturally presume that what will be tested is what will be taught.

Proponents of national testing have advocated the development of a national test for measuring reading and math achievement at three grade levels—fourth grade, eighth grade and twelfth grade. Some of these proponents would extend this national testing program to include science, history and geography. Opponents of national achievement testing argue that the consequence of the development of such tests will influence, even dictate, curriculum. Would such tests be likely to influence or dictate curriculum content in school systems choosing to adopt them? Good or bad, there is little doubt this would be true to some degree. To think otherwise would be foolish.

Suppose the tests measure skills and concepts not currently included in the curriculum. If the curriculum is not modified to include these skills and concepts, the results could be that an outstanding teacher appears to be incompetent or an outstanding school program could appear to be inferior.

Would the test administered at the fourth grade level be likely to influence or dictate the curriculum for the primary grades? Again, the answer is that there is little doubt that it would.

A school system can be expected to rate poorly on the fourth grade level test if its primary curriculum does not include the sequence of skills and concepts (prerequisites) leading to mastery of skills and concepts measured by the test. Not modifying the primary curriculum to be compatible with the fourth grade level test would be unfair to the fourth grade teacher. The results of not modifying the primary curriculum could cause an outstanding fourth grade teacher to appear to be incompetent.

Likewise, the national test administered to eighth graders will, and should, have some influence in determining curricular content for grades five through eight in school systems choosing to use it. The same will be true of the twelfth grade test in determining curricular content for grades nine through twelve.

Thus, the relationship between what is measured by a national achievement test and how such test might determine national curriculum is conceded. Does this not lead to the conclusion that a safer approach would be to:

1. determine what curricular content (skills and concepts) students should master by designated grade levels, *and then*
2. develop tests for these designated grade levels for measuring mastery of the curricular content?

The idea of first determining what curricular content students should master would appear to be a logical notion. Is it not logical that curricular content be identified before a valid test for measuring mastery of this content be developed? Asking the question from the opposite, but also logical perspective, "Can a valid test be developed before identifying what curricular content is to be measured?" Regardless of the logic of this proposed approach, it will have strong opposition. The immediate outcry from opponents will be, "Curriculum should not be dictated on a national level!"

Should The Tail Wag the Dog?

Common presumptions regarding achievement tests are that:

1. They (the tests) were developed and validated by "experts" and, therefore, must have credibility.
2. The results reveal the students' achievement levels.
3. The interpretation of the results should provide feedback data for improving or modifying the curriculum and teaching methods.

How true are these presumptions? Traditionally, standardized test developers have tended to be "experts" in research and statistics rather than curriculum "experts." Thus, they have tended to be much more concerned that their tests have statistical validity than content validity.

Commonly used standardized tests are almost notorious for their lack of content validity (Shriner and Salvia, 1988; Hargis, 1987). The items that make up tests seldom accurately represent the curriculum in use where the tests are administered. If tests are to influence or modify a curriculum, having content validity may be more crucial than statistical validity. Thus, presumption #1 above should be made with caution.

The presumption that the results from a standardized test reveals the students' achievement level (See #2 above), in many cases, can be false. For example, it is not uncommon for a school system to adopt a reading program published by one publisher and administer a state-adopted standardized reading test published by a different publisher. Thus, results derived from administering the state-adopted standardized test may or may not reveal the students' achievement level in the adopted reading program.

Likewise, the presumption that the results should provide feedback for improving or modifying the curriculum and teaching methods (See #3 above) may also be false. It may be inappropriate to let the interpretations from the state-adopted test influence what modifications are made in the adopted reading program.

Test and Curriculum Alignment

As discussed above, tests and curricula are often selected and adopted independently. Allowing school systems within a state to adopt a basal text of their choosing and then mandating a state-adopted achievement test is a common practice. The practice of mandating a state-adopted achievement text and allowing the school systems within the state to adopt a basal text usually leads to some "misalignment" between test and curricula.

The assumption is that achievement tests accurately measure learning in each area of any curriculum. Such is not the case. There is considerable misalignment. Common achievement tests seldom adequately sample items from a specific curriculum. Tests that purport to diagnose reading problems measure attributes which may not be part of the reading program in actual use with the students being tested.

The assumption is that there is some generic set of reading skills that are common to all reading curricula. Such is not the case. Reading programs vary greatly in the content, scope, and sequence of skills that they contain.

Tests are much esteemed. We give serious regard to test results. Test results gauge teachers' and schools' performance. We are concerned about improving test performance due to constant pressure from school boards and communities. It is no wonder, then, that teachers will make a direct effort to improve test scores by teaching their students specific skills and content measured in the tests they must take. When this happens, the curriculum is being aligned with the test (i.e. the tail is wagging the dog). This aligning of the curriculum with the test is not necessarily bad. However, this alignment should not be made too hastily. An evaluation should be made prior to aligning the curriculum with the test.

Before aligning the curriculum with the tests, several questions should be asked or considered:

1. Will student mastery of skills or concepts assessed by the test help the student to function more effectively and independently?
2. Why was the skill or content not included in the curricula? Should it have been?
3. Is there reason or justification to believe the skill or content is a "need to know," or is it merely a "nice to know" being added to a curricula which is already filled with more "need to knows" than most students are able to master?
4. If it is a "need to know" (higher priority skill), should it replace a "don't need to know" or "nice to know" (lower priority) skill?
5. Is there reason to believe adding the skill or content to the curricula will help the students who are not progressing well in the current curricula?

These precautions are in order as tests are often selected without regard to how well their content represents the curriculum in use.

Results may not reflect accurately actual achievement. Discrepancies or deficiencies may occur to the degree the content of the test varies from the content of the curriculum. Thus, if action to remedy what appears to be a discrepancy or deficiency are not taken with caution, the action may be inefficient or even wrong.

Standardized tests with national norms almost never contain items presented through the scope and sequence of items presented through the curricula in each of the thousands of school districts throughout the country. At best, they sample only a very few items common to most curricula at any grade level. This lack of content validity was noted earlier.

If we want content validity, if we want to measure how much of a curriculum has been learned, then the achievement test should be made up of an adequate sample of the items at each level of that curriculum. Curriculum content, what we want students to learn, must be identified first. The tests to measure progress in mastery of this content must be drawn from this content; the larger the sample drawn, the better. This insures content validity. Tests developed in this way will accurately measure how well the schools do in imparting curricular objectives to their students.

Testing and teaching, teaching and testing requires that both tests and curriculum be of the same material. Then the quality of teaching is monitored accurately, and problem areas can be accurately identified.

Tests are often selected without regard to how well their content represents the curriculum in use. Confusing and misleading information can be produced. Results may not reflect accurately actual achievement. Consequently, the actions taken to remedy poor performance are often inefficient or even wrong. Problems occur to the degree that the content of tests vary from the content of the curriculum. The routines of classroom instruction proceed along the route outlined by the flow of curricular objectives. When tests are administered and the results examined, deficiencies in test performance will typically emerge in the areas not covered by the curriculum. Test results, as mentioned earlier, are influential in redirecting instructional effort. Teachers and school officials want improved scores. The areas of deficiency, which are usually those of misalignment, will be included in instructional activity. Teachers begin to use the test as another curriculum. Two curriculums will coexist: one, the regular curriculum; the other, the test-directed curriculum. Instructional time with the regular curriculum will be reduced to the extent tests and curricula differ. Possibly the worst thing that happens is that more and more curricular items are included with simply less time for each.

Well-Chosen Tests Can Serve As a Curriculum Framework

As was just illustrated, tests can become the curriculum. This leads to some sage advice: Choose your tests well, as they (1) may become your curriculum and (2) can become a curriculum framework.

Recognizing the need for teachers to have assessments aligned with curriculum, one of the authors has developed several comprehensive tests that do just that. They are assessment procedures that are comprehensive enough to serve as curriculum guides. The assessment procedures are a "marriage" with core or basic curriculum. The two are one in the same. The curricular items are simply written in the form that resembles instructional activity.

By using the assessment procedures of the level or area which the teacher finds appropriate, the student's mastery level can be identified. The results can be used to determine the student placement in a core or basic curriculum. Thus, assessment and teaching are "tied" together as we believe they should be. Most current curricula are dominated by commercially prepared instructional programs. These programs exist for different subject areas and may have a span of several grade levels — primary, K–6, K–8, etc.

Most of these programs have a scope and sequence of curricular skills or objectives. Most include a teacher's manual for each grade level giving step-by-step directions of how the lessons for each of the 180 days are to be presented. Student materials may include textbooks, workbooks, black line masters and manipulatives. Tests for assessing student mastery after each phase or unit are often included. These tests are derived from the instructional program and thus should have adequate content validity. However, the content validity should always be questioned. This is especially true for students who have poor retention for skills which should be mastered at the automatic level. For example, results from the test may indicate student mastery for addition facts with sums 12 on Friday. However, when the student is expected to perform this mastery at a faster rate the following Wednesday, he or she is unsuccessful in doing so.

In addition to the achievement measures mentioned above, teachers are also required to test in order to give grades. They go about this in a variety of ways. They may make up their own tests, use some of the mastery tests from the instructional programs, grade homework and seatwork or use some combination of the above.

Some states and some school districts have developed basic skill curricula and tests to go with them. Teachers are required to give these, also.

Proficiency tests or minimum competency tests are in common use now. These tests set a threshold skill level in the basic subjects which the system deems necessary for graduation. Proficiency tests have a powerful influence on the direction a curriculum takes for many students (Hargis, 1990), and passing these tests is necessary for graduation. Consequently, their content directly contributes to the curriculum of many low-achieving and disadvantaged students.

Virtually all school systems give standardized achievement tests. Their influence on what teachers will include in the curriculum has already been noted. It will vary, of course, depending on how well or poorly students do on them.

When students do particularly poor on achievement tests and grade evaluations, they will be referred for diagnostic testing. Here, there are myriad tests that purport to measure every conceivable construct and aptitude that might be related to deficient achievement. When these tests are administered, deficiencies of some sort or areas of weak performance invariably will be identified. Having honored the test with credibility sufficient to administer it, we must, therefore, assume that the deficiencies so revealed must be remedied. They must be remedied since they must be the principle cause of the students' inadequate achievement. The reasoning here is that the tests are credible measures of some sort of learning problem; weakness identified on them must be the cause of the learning problem. Consequently, the remediation of these deficiencies requires a program of instruction to remove or ameliorate them. This remedial program will constitute an additional curriculum.

All of the different types of tests which we administer can form new curricula and may demand instructional time. This may cause fragmentation and confusion. The lesson to be learned is that tests must be selected or developed with care. This must be done with a curriculum in mind. If we keep the issue of curriculum and measurement in separate mental compartments, we invite the kind of bad practice just alluded to. Tests will become their own curriculum. Choose them or prepare them with much care. Curricular and measurement alignment is necessary for the most important measurement quality: content validity.

Illusive Targets Created By Standardized Tests

The emphasis on accountability and standards in recent years has created the need for a gauge or "measuring stick" to determine how well different school systems are doing. The most common gauge or measuring stick used for making this determination has been standardized, norm-referenced tests.

These standardized tests purport to measure student achievement in a manner which permits the achievement of each student or group of students to be compared with the achievement of students in a normative or "standard" population of similar students. This comparison is made possible by statistical data obtained from testing a large or well-represented sampling of a similar population.

Statistical data or indexes of performance available for the test may include standard scores, percentile ranks, stanines and grade equivalents. For some of these tests, norms are available for demographic segments of the population such as region of country, urban, rural, language, race, sex, etc. Typically, these tests are given each year, usually at the beginning or end of the school year. For continuity, the same test battery will be used over a considerable period of time. Comparisons using the same or equivalent forms of the same instrument are the most meaningful. Again, the main purpose of these tests is to serve as a common gauge or measuring stick for comparing the achievement of each student or group of students with the population used for norming. However, personnel involved in the use of these tests are sometimes tempted to extend the purpose beyond the main one for which they were intended. Yielding to this temptation may lead to using the test results inappropriately or in an abusive manner. This is likely to lead to dilemmas, problems and controversy.

One dilemma in the use of these norm-referenced instruments is that, over time, it is a common phenomenon for test scores to rise. This is enormously pleasing to the interested groups. As test scores creep up, we find that the average performance of the students currently taking the test will exceed the average established in the original standardization group. This leads to what is now being called the "Lake Wobegon Effect," that is, all the children are above average. As scores rise, school systems look with pride at the increased performance. They will make comparisons between current performance and the test norms and between current performance and past performance in the same system.

Why do scores on standardized tests tend to rise? Well, the first most obvious answer is that they rise because it is our intent and purpose as educators that we should become more effective and students should learn more. We give tests to measure our effectiveness and indicate what needs improvement. We are acting on this information, and improved test performance shows that we are.

Another reason that test performance increases is that as teachers recognize the gaps in the content validity of tests, they tend to close it. Over the years, teachers become familiar with tests. They identify items and areas that are not dealt with in their curricular pursuits. When these gaps are identified, teachers tend to add them to the curriculum and teach to them. After all, if they are important enough to include on a test, they are certainly important enough to teach, aren't they? Consequently, over time, those areas of dissimilarity between test and curriculum are closed; test scores rise.

Still another reason that test scores rise, sometimes dramatically, is that the test items themselves are being taught. The temptation to do this is considerable for a variety of reasons. It is difficult to resist the pressure to help students overcome barriers imposed by tests and to make oneself look like a gifted teacher.

In the first two instances, we would argue that actual achievement was occurring. In the last instance, nothing good was resulting. Improper practices of teachers result from using tests with poor content validity for teacher evaluation and/or student promotion.

In the first two instances, naturally rising performance may not be considered to be a legitimate increase in achievement. Critics will claim the increase in performance is only the consequence of repeated use of the same tests and norms that are getting old. These critics will apply pressure to change the tests or get a more recent edition of the same test with different items and up-to-date norms.

As the "Lake Wobegon Effect" begins to appear, critics of the schools are likely to point their fingers and exclaim, "Everyone can't be above average. These results are not valid. We will need to change and use a test published by another publisher."

When new and different tests are selected, in effect what is done is that teachers are given different objectives to achieve, a different target to aim at. Teachers are placed in a painful contradiction. If they are successful in achieving the objective of improved test performance, they are in danger of having the measure of achievement changed, the target moved.

Updated tests with new norms invariably show lower performance. Test items will be changed and their difficulty level will assure that, at least for the time being, the tests produce the desired distribution of scores for each chronological age group and grade level.

Sometimes schools are encouraged to produce local norms on these test results. If it is done each time the tests are administered, average performance will reflect only current performance. Most of the students can't be above average any longer when compared to the current norms for their own group. However, a gradual increase will be noted over the years in scores that produce each percentile rank and average performance. This is a better way to judge what average performance is than by changing the test.

One use of the test results which has produced much controversy is using the results to evaluate teacher and school effectiveness. School administration and school board members want high or improving performance on these indexes of performance. Bonuses may even be awarded based on how well students do on these tests. Classroom teachers, building principals, central administration, and the school board, all have a vested interest in high or improving performance on these tests.

It should be noted that the average performance in question is derived from current performance. It quite often is improving. The average performance currently will often exceed the average performance established in norms and for past performance in the same school system.

Fixing the Target

It is helpful to have a record of performance over time with the same tests. This information provides necessary benchmarks. We need to know where we have been and how we are doing. Merely changing the test because students are scoring better on them is unproductive as well as demoralizing. It is especially unproductive when the tests are changed without regard to content validity.

Achievement can only be measured validly by making sure that the tests accurately reflect the curriculum content the students being tested are using. The best way to make an achievement test is to take items directly from the curriculum in use. Moreover, the items should be composed in the same way they occur in regular instructional materials and activities.

More than one form can be prepared. Ideally, a pool of items from each level of the curriculum should be available so that new forms of tests can easily be assembled. Multiple, equivalent forms of tests that are respected, valid measures of progress remove the temptation to teach the content of a specific test. The teachers will feel secure in the knowledge that what they are already teaching is what will be measured. The testing program will no longer present illusive moving targets.

What Should We Teach, and What Should We Test?

Will the consequence of the current debate on national educational standards and testing help us focus on what we should teach? Will it lead to tests that measure what we should teach?

The attention to standards and tests should help us try to identify those things that are most important to teach and, consequently, to measure to see if they have been learned. A more useful alignment of tests and curriculum should emerge. Teaching to the test will become the logical and intelligent outcome. The curriculum should be altered to include content and skills of greatest importance or priority. The development of tests for assessing mastery of this curriculum should follow. This all sounds rather simple. Surely, it will be easy to identify the content and skills students should be learning. Isn't there already consensus on what should be learned in most subject areas?

Actually, there is little consensus in any subject area. Even mathematics, a seemingly neutral area, has been plagued with variability and controversy. Theories about what elements of mathematics should be taught, and how and when they should be taught, continue to make math curricula a stew of content.

There are three perspectives on what the math curriculum should contain. These are the basic skills position, the understanding or "new math" position, and the social utility or life skill position. The relative influence of each position on curricular content is not static but shifts with the prevailing mood in the country.

Two of the positions are nearly in opposition. The skill-versus-understanding debate has been going on since early in the century. Those who would emphasize computational algorithms and problem-solving skills are on one side and those who emphasize "understanding" and "meaningful" instruction on the other. The latter group is associated with the "new math" and is linked with the period from the late 1950s to the late 1970s. The former group is associated with the "back-to-basics" movement.

Preceding the skill-versus-understanding controversy by many years, and still exerting influence in some sectors, is the social utility influence. It goes under a variety of titles, such as consumer math, life skill math, practical math, and survival math. A renewed emphasis emerges here each time testing or observation points out that students can't handle day-to-day math problems such as balancing a checkbook, figuring sales tax, or making change, even after completing one or the other of the previously mentioned curricula. Advocates of practical math have been around since Ben Franklin used the notion to promote the teaching of arithmetic.

These perspectives have dramatically different influences on curriculum development. One group wants elements of higher math concepts taught from the beginning of the primary grades. They claim that the math curriculum is being "dumbed down" unless set theory, geometry, and algebra are taught in the primary grades. Another group claims the students are deficient in basic computational skills and the curriculum needs to focus on fundamentals. The third group says that students must be taught at least those math skills that they will need in order to do functional computation for success in daily living.

Each of these groups has a very different view as to what scope and sequence of skills should make up a K–12 curriculum. Obviously, tests measuring progress along each of them will, of necessity, be composed quite differently.

The field of reading is similarly comprised of conflicting views on how reading instruction should proceed. The objectives to be attained and the content and skills that are to be presented at each grade level are fundamentally different. In past years, the amount and type of word identification (phonic) skills separated the camps. The commercially prepared basal reading programs dominated the curriculum used to teach reading. Today, another position has emerged, the "whole language" philosophy, which poses an entirely different approach to reading instruction in the elementary grades. Needless to say, curricular content and tests will be remarkably different.

The teaching of history depends largely on the content of texts used to teach it. What historical items are essential or relevant are currently being debated. Also, arguments over dissembling and revisionism are rampant among historians.

Experts and critics often claim that our students are not learning how to learn or how to think. We should emphasize problem-solving ability, communication skill, reasoning, understanding concepts, attitudes, motivation, and learning style. These constructs are not specifically defined. They are theoretical. Their theoretical and even arcane definitions make it difficult to produce valid test items to measure them. When tests for them are prepared, it is done independently of any curriculum. Consequently, content validity is questionable. There is pressure to test some of these constructs diagnostically, and when they are, they will influence the curriculum because of the prescription the results will inevitably imply.

In sum, there is no non-controversial curricular area. Will national curricular standards and tests emerge? We will have to wait and see. However, the attempt is useful. Constantly, reflection on what we should teach should help us bring into focus what we should be teaching and how we should be assessing what is taught.

More attention does need to be focused on what skills should be assessed. Too often, tests are constructed without much regard to relevance of items. Unfortunately, of more concern to test constructors is the construction of tests with items that have various degrees of discriminating power for the purpose of producing a normal distribution of scores.

Continually reflecting on what we should teach and test should lead to the construction of authentic tests with more content validity. The development of these tests should help us focus on the curriculum and help us clarify what is important for us to teach.

Authentic testing with good content validity measures learning in the way it occurs in the classroom. Tests with these qualities are made up of the activities and materials that make up the ongoing instructional activities. Striving for authenticity and content validity in our testing also helps us to reflect on how we are doing the teaching as well as how we are constructing our tests. If our tests are simply a list of multiple-choice items, it already indicates a lack of authenticity. If multiple-choice tests are authentic, in other words reflect multiple-choice teaching, then the format of instruction certainly must be of questionable quality.

Testing and the Lock-Step Curriculum

Universal, free public education began in this country concurrent with our rapid period of industrialization. The development of standardization, interchangeable parts, and the factory system was as dominant an influence on mass education as it was on mass production. The old subscription schools with the multi-age mixes, with teachers dealing with instruction at every level and on all subjects began to disappear. The graded system, where children were grouped with chronological age peers so that instruction could be meted out more efficiently to very large numbers of students, began to emerge, especially in densely populated urban areas. Students in the old subscription schools stayed in school until they had learned as much as their teachers had to impart or until they reached a satisfactory level of literacy, or a plateau that they could not surpass.

In the newer graded system, which developed rapidly after the Civil War, students moved through each step or grade until they could proceed no further or they came to the end of the available grades, 6, 8, 10, or 12. The extension of public education through the high school level came around the turn of the century. The standard 12 grades was virtually universal by the end of World War II. Mandatory attendance to a certain age was instituted in most states in the 1930s. Students were required to continue in school, even if they were not progressing with their chronological-age peers, until they reached the legal age, usually 16 or 17. The old, ungraded schools (there are still such schools in rural and sparsely populated areas) permitted students to progress, plateau, or finish at their own pace.

The graded system, however, typically could not allow for individual pacing. The curriculum was apportioned for each grade. That portion assigned to each grade was further apportioned to a sequence fitting over the academic year that formed the boundaries of every grade. All students were expected to "march" through the lock-step sequence with their chronological-age peers. If they couldn't manage the pace and failed to keep up, they received failing grades. Grades, this time letter grades, were an artifact of the new system. Students were being graded even more. Their place was now being established relative to their chronological-age peers within each grade level.

Those students who can't keep the pace on the lock-step march through the curriculum fail. Failure to make progress results in retention. A student who makes no progress often repeats the grade. Repeating grades is a common occurrence in the lock-step system. Students who ultimately drop out usually have repeated one or more grades. Being behind, and without prospects for finishing, they leave school. This happens to roughly 25 percent of students who begin the K through 12 march (Kronick and Hargis, 1990).

In effect, the curriculum itself poses a test, a form of timed test. Those students who perform adequately on curricular activities assigned to each of the 180 days in their grade continue to "march" along the lock-step. However, about three or four students in every classroom will be unable to perform well and will fail. Indeed, failing grades on routine curricular work is a primary diagnostic assessment procedure.

How is it that a curriculum can behave like a test, producing a distribution of grades and scores in the students who engage in it? It is in the diverse nature of the students. We have the erroneous notion that if we group children with their chronological-age peers, that the students in each group will have similar academic abilities or readiness levels with which to begin instruction at each grade level.

Actually, chronological age is an extremely poor indicator of academic aptitude. It is, however, the primary gauge we use. We assume there should be no more variation in learning aptitude, or achievement, in each grade than there is in chronological age, which is 12 months. The actual range in achievement is far greater than the range of chronological age. This is true even if we eliminate the least able and the most able students, those who could be considered exceptional, either handicapped or gifted, by some definition. This is illustrated in the table below (Hargis, 1990). The range in reading achievement for grades 1 through 4 is reported in grade-equivalent scores. It reports the range in reading achievement, excluding the bottom and the top 5 percent of the students in each grade. This is an overly conservative estimate of achievement in each grade level, but it will serve to emphasize the normal variation that we should expect.

Range of Reading Grade Placement (G.P.) Scores for Grades 1 Through 4

Grade in School	1st	2nd	3rd	4th
Low G.P. Score	0.5	1.1	1.9	2.5
High G.P. Score	3.4	5.3	7.1	8.7
Range in G.P.	2.9	4.2	5.2	6.2

Not incidentally, this range in achievement for each grade level can be verified by examining the normative data from the reading portion of any popular standardized achievement test. It will be reconfirmed with any updating of norms as long as we have chronological age grouping by grades.

Notice, from this simple table, that the range in reading achievement at the end of first grade will be 2.9 years. This is about three times the range in chronological age. By the end of the second grade the range increases to 4.2 years. The range in achievement increases by about a year at each succeeding grade level. By the end of the fourth grade it has more than doubled.

We are misled by the central tendencies, the averages, and the continued stability of the range in chronological age. The average reading achievement will continue to be at the grade level. It is the range that increases. Notice, also, that the amount of increase in achievement is, of course, one year for each grade level at the average. However, the increase in achievement is only a little over .5 year for the lower-achieving students, while it is more than 1.5 years for the higher ones.

Thus, the rate of achievement for the higher-achieving students is about three times as fast as it is for the lower students. Lower-achieving students are falling farther and farther behind their average chronological-age peers, while the higher-achieving ones are moving increasingly farther in advance of them.

The extremes of normal variation in achievement were not considered in the above illustration. Actually, teachers in primary grades are likely to have students who perform in both ends of this achievement continuum in their classrooms every year. After all, they represent 10 percent of the population, or 2–3 of every class of 25 students. The lower-achieving students (the lowest 5 percent) seldom survive very long in regular classrooms and are usually placed in special education classrooms.

The array of individual differences in achievement remains remarkably wide. We clearly do not confront this fact; the curriculum only provides one level of instruction geared to the average learning rate of the chronological-age group assigned to each grade. About two-thirds of the students assigned to each grade can perform adequately in the curriculum. This fact gives us the notion that if that many students can do adequate work in a lock-step curriculum, then there must be something wrong with those students who can't. We have come to view normal variation in academic ability and learning efficiency as a malady that must be cured with the help of further testing.

Testing to Cure Individual Differences

Each fall, children with the normal diverse range in academic readiness and potential line up outside first grade classrooms. Can we expect them all to benefit in equal measure from the instructional program to be offered during the next nine months? The lock-step curriculum suggests this is our expectation. Our experience, and findings such as illustrated above, clearly indicate we cannot expect all students to benefit in equal measure. We can expect students whose learning aptitude and facility at learning are lowest (those below the 5th percentile) to benefit the least. Some of these will be referred for services and placement and services. Some of those referred will be administered a battery of tests, possibly including an individual intelligence test, to see if they can qualify for placement in special education programs. Depending on factors such as state and local requirements and funding, 3 to 10 percent may qualify for placement in special education. We know that many more students than this fail to learn in the regular classroom. Ultimately, 15 to 30 percent will fail to complete school, and for most of these students, failure and retention mark the history of their time spent in school.

Some children with obvious difficulty in learning in the lock-step cannot immediately qualify for special education. Their learning rates and skill levels are just a little better than those in the mildly mentally retarded groups, but not close enough to the threshold required for normal achievement progress.

The learning rates of this group is from 15 to 40 percent slower than for those students at the average. They are starting at a disadvantage and the pace of instruction leaves them farther and farther behind each year. This mismatch of ability and instructional load compounds the learning problem. These students are increasingly less able to learn up to their own potential. The curricular burden becomes increasingly heavier due to the pace of instruction. Newly introduced material is added to the still unlearned load the students already bare.

Eventually, a gap develops between a student's achievement and potential for achievement. When the gap reaches a significant proportion, the student qualifies as *learning disabled*. This discrepancy procedure is a fairly common one for qualifying students for special education services under the learning disabilities label. We believe the label is inappropriate for most of the students that receive it. Most are normal students whose only problem is their learning rates are out of synchronization with the lock-step curriculum. We prefer the label *curriculum casualty* (Hargis, 1982, 1987).

We will not deny that there are a substantial number of students with genuine learning problems caused by an organic origin within the student.

However, we believe that the clear majority of students identified as learning disabled are really curriculum casualties.

The assessment procedure for separating the actual learning disabled from the curriculum casualty is quite straightforward. Unfortunately, it is seldom used. The procedure will be described in detail later, but it is essentially this: The curricular material that students are failing in is adjusted to fit their skill level and learning rate. If failure ends and the behaviors associated with learning disabilities cease, then the students are curriculum casualties; the lock-step curriculum is at fault. If, however, the match between student and curriculum can't be made with consistent success on the student's part and the behaviors persist, then the student is likely to have a real learning disability. Special education may be indicated if the management of the student's problems can't be taken care of with appropriate support.

All too often we treat the symptom rather than the cause of the learning problem. This is the reason that the simple diagnostic procedure mentioned two paragraphs above is almost never used. However, it should always be the first stage of assessment for children with suspected or assumed learning disabilities.

When children are confronted with schoolwork that is of appropriate difficulty (i.e. not too many unknown words in reading, not too many new facts in math), they will engage in doing it. They will be engaged and completing their work successfully. This appropriate level is known as the instructional level. Much more will be said about it and its importance to assessment throughout the book. The instructional level permits students to successfully engage in schoolwork.

The instructional, frustration, and basal levels of difficulty were defined by Emmett Betts (1946) for reading instruction. The instructional and frustration levels for other curricular areas are explained by Hargis (1987, 1989, 1990). Again, these levels are very important to educational assessment and will be reviewed in detail in later chapters. If the difficulty level of schoolwork exceeds the appropriate instructional level, it becomes frustrating for the student. This level is called the frustration level.

The point at which the difficulty level of schoolwork moves from instructional level to frustration level is also the point where many behaviors associated with the learning disabled appear. If work is too difficult to engage in with reasonable success, the student is very likely to show signs of frustration and go off task. It is very hard to attend to work that is too difficult, and, consequently, behaviors associated with attention deficits develop. The symptom is assumed to be the cause. The curricular difficulty factor is ignored, and a curriculum devoted to improving the attending behaviors may be instituted. In some cases, a drug may even be prescribed to aid the student's attending power.

A variety of behaviors can emerge, especially with chronic frustration; some children spend years in school trying to cope with frustration level work. The children who are by nature more assertive may engage in more disruptive, annoying behaviors. Students who are by nature shy and reticent will withdraw and avoid the painful work, possibly engaging in daydreaming and doodling. This latter group is more likely to be ignored. Both groups deserve much better treatment than they get.

The relationship between the difficulty of a task and the ability to stay engaged in it is curvilinear. In other words, if schoolwork is too difficult, students can't stay with it because they can't really engage in it. As the task becomes easier, then engaged time increases. However, as the difficulty level passes the point of appropriateness to the point of needless repetition of mastered material, engaged time falls off again. This is the passage from good work to busy work.

The lock-step curriculum provides the learning environment that produces this behavior curve. The single level of instruction induces the curve in engaged time at every grade level. Most of the off-task behavior in classrooms can be attributed to this. Many academically talented students will suffer some discomfort from this condition and will have their achievement performance squelched to the extent that they lack educational resources at home.

Norms and the Curriculum

Traditionally, testing and assessment have focused on determining how well a student or a group of students perform relative to an identified group of students. This identified group typically consists of a group of students of the same chronological age—the group or population used for establishing norms for the test. Does this focus offer the best means for improving curriculum? Does this focus promote the alignment of assessment and curriculum?

A more productive focus would be on determining how well a student or a group of students are progressing on a specific curriculum, preferably a curriculum designed to meet the needs of the student(s). Rather than yielding a score, rank, percentile, etc., the assessment should identify the achievement or mastery level on the continuum of the curriculum.

In order to accomplish this, the assessment items must be constructed in a format and manner as close as possible to the format in which it is taught—authentic assessment. The information gained from such tests should place a student with good precision on the continuum of the curriculum. This information should help start or continue instruction at an appropriate instructional level on the curriculum. It also tells with substance what the student has learned.

Normative, as opposed to substantive, testing simply tells how a student has done when compared to others in her or his grade when taking a particular test. None of the scores or indexes of performance tell, with anything approaching adequate precision, what a student has learned. Only if the test content itself has been integrated in the curricular offering will it begin to have content validity.

Normative tests help perpetuate the use of the lock-step curriculum. We have learned to expect the kind of scores from these tests that tell us how given children are doing compared to others in their grade. The curriculum itself is normative. It is apportioned to each grade according to how well "typical" students in those grades should perform in it. Never mind that there will be students in every grade that are "normally" achieving both below and above the grade designation.

The lock-step of grades and curriculum also permit us to use our normative grading procedures. When the diverse group of students in each grade is compelled to work in the same curriculum assigned to it, a distribution of grades will result. Some teachers will fit them to the "normal" curve, 7-24-38-24-7: 7 percent each for A's and F's, 24 percent each for B's and D's, and 38 percent for C's.

In some classrooms a scale such as this one may be used: 93–100, A; 85–92, B; 77–84, C; 70–76, D; 0–69, F. Again, given the single level of instruction, a range of scores will result. This range of performance will simply reflect how much each student was an engaged participant in the learning activities in that classroom. These kinds of normative comparisons are institutionalized. We seem to have learned to need these comparative, normative measures. We overlook the fact that much devastation is done to students because of these normative procedures. Most of our problems are really casualties of this system.

Standardization procedures should be applied to curricular items, not to student performance. We need to pay far more attention to the selection and positioning of items on the curriculum. Curricular content should be ordered in a sequence that is developmental, from simple to complex, from concrete to abstract, etc. Attention should be given to the readiness relationships of preceding and subsequent steps.

It is important to consider carefully what it is we want to teach, and it is equally important to place curricular items in a hierarchy of difficulty that makes them teachable. Both tests and curriculum should be prepared with this in mind. They should be prepared in a complimentary, content-valid way, not as independent and unrelated program elements.

Chapter 2

SUCCESS AND FAILURE

Educational testing is usually performed to obtain a normative index of a student's achievement or of a group of students. This index is to show the relative position of a student or students with grade or age level peers. The most commonly reported indexes on standardized tests are percentiles and grade equivalents.

Letter grades are the most common index of the routine tests given by teachers. Teachers test routinely through the school year. They enter scores or grades in grade books and then calculate final grades for courses. The grades are based on how well grade level peers perform on a given test, determined by either percent correct or a normative curve.

Students taking these tests are simply measured to produce an index, the scores or percentiles. We then arrange these indexes on continuum from lowest to highest or fail to excellent.

Tests have the wrong focus. They rank and label. Most tests don't provide real help. They produce only letters or numbers. We seem to be willing to measure only to compare, either to others or to the scale of items on a test. There is currently developing a movement toward more authentic, substantive forms of measurement, however. Authentic measurement concerns itself with what students have actually learned. More will be said about this authentic or performance-based assessment later. There is also movement toward a more active form of assessment that concerns itself with student success. It is not the old passive measurement that only provides a number or index for comparison. It is a dynamic, substantive form of assessment that is used to insure that students succeed. It is this concern with success that is different and important. It is a form of assessment that is an active ingredient in the instructional process and has as its central concern maintaining students at success level performance. Much more will be said about success-based assessment throughout this book.

Why do we have this concern with success? We have developed this concern with success primarily because of its opposite: failure. For many years we have dealt with the devastating consequences of failure and have concluded that it must be consciously avoided through planned measurement and instructional practice. Assessment must become an active process. Success must become assessment's central concern. The focus should be on confirming success or to identify reason(s) for the lack of success.

The Double Standard

There is a gross misperception held by many critics of our educational system. It is that poor achievement is the result of our failure to challenge students. They feel that if teachers would only hold higher standards for the lower-achieving students, they would perform up to grade level. The critics feel we should demand more, not less. We should not "dumb down" the curricular activities for lower-achieving students. They feel that lower achievement is actually the result of our low expectations and practice.

We feel this thinking is fundamentally flawed. We feel that, if anything, many students are challenged far too much and that raising expectations will cause more frustration. Lower-achieving students, unfortunately, are almost always failing. They are challenged far beyond their capacity. Their routine work is at the frustration level, far more challenging than an appropriate instructional level.

On the other hand, the higher-achieving students are seldom challenged to this extent. Their work is routinely at a more appropriate instructional level. Notable are the high comprehension and fluency in reading, the high scores and grades on other routine work. A comfortable level of challenge permits high performance and an easy route to mastery.

Lower-achieving students are overly challenged. They encounter far too many unknowns in their reading, seatwork, and homework activities. Red marks cover their papers indicating the high degree of failure. Buckets of red ink are wasted to demonstrate the extent to which these students are failing. The use of this red ink reflects the symptom and not the cause. It does not reflect the degree to which these students are confronted with instruction at their frustration level and beyond. We have a serious double standard in our schools. We have the misconception that we should challenge the unfortunate students who are not doing well. There are claims that these poor students would do better if only we would expect more of them. These claims are made without regard to the fact that for higher-achieving students we permit ease, comfort, and success by assigning appropriate instructional level challenge. High-achieving students get the reinforcing benefits of success and progress, while their lower-achieving peers get the aversive effect of failure and frustration. This double standard should be eliminated.

The fallacy of unreasonable expectations perpetuates this double standard. Further, it is used as a justification for not individualizing instruction. Instead of presenting instruction at their instructional level, instruction is presented at grade level. Even if the student tries to perform, too frequently the result is failure.

The fallacy is based on the assumption that everyone can and should work at grade level. If they are not, then the reason they are not is that we don't hold high enough expectations for them. Expecting students to do schoolwork that is too difficult, along with a low level of motivation, is what causes failure. Students do not willingly and voluntarily fail. Failure is imposed on them by imposing grade level standards which are above their instructional level. Imposing these standards creates a failure pool. This failure pool is primarily comprised of the disadvantaged—students with limited academic potential and limited motivations for academic achievement.

As was illustrated in the previous chapter, we should always expect a range in instructional level skills that extends far below and far above actual grade placement. This normal range of ability is not a malady, curable by expecting all students to do grade level work. Our expectation should be that all students be placed at the highest instructional level at which they can perform with the same comfort as their high-achieving peers. Appropriate challenging expectations can be ascertained through measurement. These systems will be detailed later. In short, they identify the highest instructional level for students where learning can occur successfully and efficiently. These expectation levels should be individually determined. They should be based on accurate assessment information.

Our expectations should not be governed by what any student's age or grade peers are doing. We should not expect the same thing for all students. We should expect them to be successful in the work we provide them. They should be challenged at the highest level on the curriculum where they can work with the comfort and pleasure that instills the enjoyment of learning. We should learn to expect students to be working at many different levels, but with the same level of success. We must have the same standard for all students—the standard of success.

Success and Achievement

Nothing breeds success like success. This is only one of the many familiar aphorisms concerning the benefits of success. We seem to know intuitively that success is better than failure. However, this intuitiveness seems to become passive in our schools. This passivity is brought about in part by our lock-step curriculum in which some failure is the "norm." We propose that success be planned for all students. We propose that assessment procedures which assure success become the focus of our educational system. We propose a new metric, one that does not simply sort or rank students according to where they are relative to their chronological age or grade peers.

To understand the importance of success, it is necessary to understand the devastating effects of failure. In simple terms, students are failing when too many answers on their tests or homework are wrong. However, in order to learn the correct answers, they must be getting the correct answers. Too many wrong answers indicates more than just a poor grade. It is evidence that students are being overwhelmed with material they do not understand, cannot practice correctly, and consequently cannot learn.

Too many wrong answers tells also that corrective feedback is not possible because there is too much to correct for the feedback to be of any benefit. Students who are failing are overwhelmed at both sides. Too much is too hard, and when they get it wrong, there is too much to correct with any benefit.

Chronic failure may teach the student to give up when encountering instructional tasks (Grimes, 1981). Students facing continued failure learn to be helpless. They learn the easiest way to avoid the misery of failure is by not continuing to try, by not continuing to fill in the blanks with the wrong answers. This failure and not continuing to try is often directly related to emotional and behavioral problems. Failure is damaging to self-esteem. Students need reasonable amounts of success in order to develop confidence and a sense of competence. Failure prevents the development of a sense of competence and confidence and damages the student's self-concept.

Self-esteem is not something we can develop in students in order to prevent failure. The reverse is true. We must prevent failure in order to enhance confidence and self-esteem. Problems with self-esteem abound in children. To damage it further by permitting, or even requiring failure, is foolhardy. Failure is not confidence-building at any age. Failure is nonproductive or worse in regard to achievement. It will prevent students from achieving to their potential for achievement. This discrepancy between potential and achievement becomes greater the longer failure continues.

Failure and the Learning Disabled Scenario

In many states the discrepancy between potential and achievement is used as part of the criteria for identifying students as learning disabled. The dimension of the discrepancy that qualifies the students as learning disabled does vary from state to state. However, this discrepancy is typically so major students are required to endure the pain of failure for an extended amount of time prior to being classified as learning disabled and qualifying for services.

The unfortunate thing about this definition of learning disabilities is that it requires a great deal of failure in order to achieve it. For many students, the time required for developing this discrepancy can be a long and painful period.

The rationale for this procedure is that if students are achieving close to their potential, their learning ability cannot be considered impaired. What constitutes a significant discrepancy varies state by state, but the measures of aptitude and achievement are similar.

An individual test of intelligence is used as the measure of aptitude or potential for achievement, and a standardized achievement test is used as the measure of achievement.

The method of calculating the discrepancy varies, but the discrepancy must be of substantial proportions. For example, if a ten-year-old student had an IQ score of 100, he or she could be expected to achieve like the average ten-year-old fifth grader. However, if he or she had an achievement level at the fourth grade level, then there would be a full year's discrepancy between the student's potential for achievement and actual achievement as measured by the tests used.

In many states or programs the degree of discrepancy required for receiving special education services is greater than indicated in this example. Discrepancy definitions of learning disabilities have the negative effect of making failure seem a legitimate activity. They require failure for extended periods in order for the discrepancy to be produced. The ten-year-old mentioned will likely have been living with failure in school for his or her entire school experience until this discrepancy reaches the required magnitude.

This ten-year-old may gain relief from failure by gaining the label *learning disabled.* It is exactly this process that has created the flood of children into special education classrooms. These children are failure-caused learning disabled students (Hargis and Terhaar-Yonkers, 1989). They constitute the clear majority of students identified or classified as the learning disabled.

Of the many children who do poor and failing work, the group who eventually gets the learning disabled label may well be considered the fortunate ones. They may get some relief in the haven of special education. Despite the negativeness of the label, the freedom from failure is a genuine respite.

Failure and the Dropout Scenario

Many students doing poorly and experiencing failure in school do not meet the criteria to be identified as learning disabled. Some of these students make marginal progress, but their level of achievement does not qualify them for special services. The function of some of these students may be functioning at the borderline level for meeting the discrepancy for the learning disabled, but limited space and funding for this program may not permit placement.

For this group, the scenario is different from that of the learning disabled scenario explained above. This group of students must continue to endure the painful failure until they reach the legal age to drop out. While waiting to reach the legal dropout age, some of this group develop emotional and behavior problems as a result of chronic failure. These problems frequently disrupt the learning process of these students as well as other students.

Eventually, these students reach an age at which they can legally drop out of school. Without the prospects for passing the required courses, some manage to disappear prior to reaching the legal dropout age. This group of students constitutes the vast majority of students who drop out of school (Kronick and Hargis, 1990).

We have seldom found low-achieving students surviving in high school, let alone making achievement progress that matches their capacity. Typically, those that manage to survive have compensatory skills or characteristics that help them hang on. These include athletic, musical, mechanical, or artistic talents that make students feel they have a place in school. A few students survive because of some endearing personality characteristic. However, none of these survivors are avoiding failure or increasing achievement.

What "triggers" this failure scenario? The causes are multifaceted and varied. For some students, their failure may be "triggered" by out-of-school factors which hamper school performance. This may include a family crisis such as a death in the family or a divorce of the parents. For others, there are health problems, including nutritional problems, which may cause absenteeism or a low energy level. For the adolescent, there may be a personal crisis, which may include the use of drugs or alcohol, peer competition or rejection which is usually a very sensitive matter for this age group, and, yes, problems related to sex.

There are often in-school factors or causes. We have previously mentioned the lock-step curriculum and the failure caused by forcing students with diverse learning abilities into it. However, the specific reasons for failure have to do with the difficulty of specific tasks that make up schoolwork. A task is too difficult if it has too many unknown parts, too many parts requiring skills that are not yet learned by the individual student confronted by it.

There may be too many unknown words in a reading selection. A student cannot both identify all the words and comprehend the passage. In an arithmetic task, a problem may require subskills that a student has not yet mastered. An assignment may introduce more new information than a student can manage to store in his or her short-term memory.

Failure, Scores and Grading

Failure can be described by various cutoff scores that are arbitrary or subjective. It is often a subjective decision where an "F" should be positioned on a grading scale. Should it be at 70, 69, 65, 64, or 59 percent correct? Can partial credit be given for a problem that is to some extent done correctly? If F's are assigned to a portion of a distribution calculated on a normal distribution, the placement could be either generous, brutal, or anyplace in between, depending on the difficulty of a test and the ability of the students.

For example, if a test were very difficult, the scores might be very low. The mean for the test might be 50 percent or less correct. In these instances an F would be assigned to a much lower score, while an A could be assigned to a percentage as low or lower than that level that would be assigned an F on a fixed standard. If, on the other hand, the scores were all skewed to the high end of the percentage scale, a grade of F could well be assigned to a level that would be that of a C or B on a fixed scale.

Both possibilities outlined above reflect poor but common practices in assigning grades. They are both only arbitrarily reflective of failure. The most objective measure of determining the boundaries between failure and success have come from some of the literature on curriculum-based assessment.

This more objective measure of failure relates the difficulty of a task to a student's ability to remain engaged in doing it. When a task becomes so difficult that a student can't remain mentally engaged in doing it, learning ceases and the threshold of failure has been reached.

Emmett Betts (1946) first described this point in reading difficulty, the point at which the reading material becomes too hard to engage in. We will discuss this point later in the chapter. In drill and seatwork activities, there is also a point at which students begin to fall off task and show the signs of frustration that are common to the threshold of failure. This point will also be discussed later.

Fundamentally and objectively, failure occurs when the difficulty of a task becomes sufficiently great that students' capacities to engage in it is exceeded and learning no longer can go on. Actually, some learning may go on, but not of a fruitful kind. Students are in danger of learning wrong answers, and they are certainly learning to dislike and avoid these frustrating tasks. In many cases students are learning helplessness.

Students constantly confronted with failure level tasks may resort to purposeless, random guessing. They have insufficient known context in reading to make anything more than a random guess as to what each of the too many unknown words are. They will be so overwhelmed by unknown words that the use of decoding skills will be needed constantly and the reading rate will be reduced nearly to a standstill of painful word-by-word sounding out, a behavior labeled *word calling*.

In math activities, there is a great risk of learning wrong answers. In drill or practice activities students have the opportunity to repeat wrong answers. As wrong answers are practiced, wrong answers are learned. Error patterns emerge through the practice of erroneous response strategies, some of which may have started as random guesses. Eventually, these are learned response patterns, and they cause many more problems than not knowing an answer at all.

Activities that are provided to students for practice should be made up, for the most part, of items that they can do correctly but not yet quickly, easily, or automatically. Students should not have the opportunity to practice errors. Failure level work often provides more opportunity for practicing errors than practicing correct responses leading to mastery.

Continued failure produces a variety of learned error patterns and negative or ineffective approaches to learning. Consequently, students that experience failure for extended periods often require remedial instruction. Remedial instruction is time consuming and labor intensive. The behaviors these students have learned must be identified, unlearned, and then replaced by the appropriate response or procedure. Identifying the many different error patterns can be a difficult, occasionally mystifying, problem. The reason for these problems is having to practice at the failure level. Failure should be avoided to prevent the need for time-consuming remedial instruction. Written composition poses especially difficult problems. Standards used to evaluate written expression are the most arbitrary and varied. The unreliability and variability of teacher judgment has been well known since Starch and Elliot (1912) performed their classic study. Further, the use of normative judgments compound the problem for many students.

When students attempt written composition, they are often overwhelmed by the many red marks and poor grades they receive. There will be so many places where the students are marked off that they will not likely benefit from correction. There will be just too many different problems marked for them to fruitfully focus on. The students may feel no hope for success in written composition and so attempt to avoid the activity completely. Success at written composition is illusive because of the ambiguous standards, but more so because the standards may be arbitrarily high.

Lower-achieving students will make many more mistakes than their higher-achieving peers. In order to avoid the frustration, they feel each time they produce written composition they may limit and restrict their output so that there will be less material to be criticized. They may also attempt to cheat, getting others to write for them or plagiarizing results. Failure for these students means less and less practice on a skill that requires a great deal of practice with much reasonable, helpful feedback.

The Need for Effective Practice

Since they are working at frustration and failure levels, lower-achieving students are denied the essential practice necessary to achieve mastery and fluency in math, reading, and writing activities. Useful practice is seldom possible for low achievers. Practice should be done with facts and skills that are understood but have not yet reached the level of mastery that make them fluent and automatic. Practice is needed for the transition of words, facts, and skills from short-term to long-term memory. Low-achieving students cannot make the transition to long-term memory; too many newly introduced unknowns are piling up with the previously introduced but still unlearned items. These are overwhelming demands on the memory and learning capacity of these students. Practice or repetition is only effective if, at each repetition, students are able to connect the right response to the item. If the response is wrong, the students learn nothing, or worse, learns the wrong answer.

"The more you do, the more you can do," is another old aphorism related to success. More specifically it means, the more you engage effectively in an activity, the better you get at it. This is true until you reach the limit of your talent. It is as true of learning to read as it is of learning to play golf, to play a musical instrument, or do mechanical work. The reverse is also true. If you engage in an activity poorly and ineffectively, you are very unlikely to improve your performance and you may get worse.

Matthew Effects

The phenomena just mentioned are ascribable to another old aphorism, "The rich get richer and the poor get poorer." There has been some interest recently in this phenomenon as it applies to education. The phenomenon is called Matthew effects (Stanovich, 1986; Hargis, Terhaar-Yonkers, Reed, and Williams, 1988).

Matthew effects work in learning to read in the following ways: Those students who are acquiring reading skill find opportunities for reading opening all around them. Printed messages are everywhere. Reading is used in all the school subjects. A wealth of reading opportunities becomes available for the students who succeed. Countless opportunities for practice reading occur everywhere. As words are learned, these same words provide the contextual base for learning more words. It appears that reading ability increases in the most able students in an explosion that exceeds by far the rate at which reading instruction proceeds. These students appear to be teaching themselves to read, and in many respects they are.

On the poor-get-poorer side, however, students who fail appear to make little or no progress and seem to get worse over time. These students cannot benefit from the wealth of incidental opportunities for reading practice that surround them. They are not able to use reading in other subject areas. They cannot read for pleasure. They fall farther and farther behind their higher-achieving peers and, worse, farther and farther behind their own potential. They feel increasingly frustrated, helpless, and ineffective which further compounds their problems.

This kind of failure is an institutionalized part of our educational system. We expect failure; it is a part of our grading system. Failure is our principle diagnostic tool. Students must fail and do so substantially before anything is done. What is often done is only an attempt to fit the students back into the system. Efforts are not directed to the real problem, which is failure. The most common intervention is retention, requiring students to repeat grades. This is done in the old lock-step without regard to what the students' specific instructional levels might be. Failure is not a precise measure; it is only crude and cruel. An effective educational measurement system must not include this crude metric. We must exchange it for a more sensitive index that guides us to appropriate instructional levels and success.

An often overlooked and undervalued principle of learning is that success is its most important ingredient. A learner must get the correct answer. The conditions for getting the correct answer must become the conscious strategy for teaching all children, not just the higher-achieving ones who happen to benefit from an alignment with the curriculum that is at their instructional level.

The success metric must be applied constantly to insure success. All instructional activities should be appraised in this way. Assessment should be part and parcel of all instructional activity. This is the approach advocated in some forms of curriculum-based assessment (Hargis, 1987, 1990). Any activity that is usually evaluated for the purpose of giving a grade should instead be evaluated in terms of its difficulty for the student. For example, give each student no more spelling words to practice at the beginning of the week than he or she can learn with near

100 percent accuracy on Friday. The same is true for any other activity or item being introduced and practiced.

Usually, however, evaluation on routine activities is used for giving grades to students. All the students will be given the same list of 20 spelling words to practice, and on Friday's test there will be a range of performance which will permit the assignment of a range of grades. One level of difficulty usually will induce a distribution of scores, unless its level of difficulty is below that of the least able or above that of the most able students.

It would surprise no one that some students do poorly and some do very well on the 20-word spelling test. This passive evaluation for the purpose of grading does not help produce the success match needed to maximize the learning of each student. Assessment should help us find the maximum instructional load at which each student can work with a level of success that means learning is going on at the most efficient level. More simply put, if a student is given 20 words to learn on Monday but gets only 5 correct on Friday, we must assume that he has been given too many words to learn. Instead of giving this student 20 words, a trial should be started to see how many words the student can master by week's end. It likely will be found that he may manage fewer words with a far higher success rate than before. It might well be that he can double the number of words mastered if he is given half the number to learn in the first place.

The same condition may be true at the opposite end of the continuum. Twenty words might be a lighter load than necessary for some. Possibly 30 or more words could be mastered with little additional effort. The point of both cases is that the index of success is the metric which must dominate routine educational assessment. All students should benefit from the use of a standard based on success rather than on norms and averages. The students at both ends of the achievement continuum benefit.

Failure and poor performance accounts for the range of underachievement and the emergence of the discrepancy between achievement and potential. We must keep in mind that poor performance and failure are not usually the fault of the students; they are the result of the lock-step curriculum and the normative forms of assessment that are an integral part of it.

Remember, however, that success does not cure individual differences. Differences in achievement are naturally quite wide and the range continues to widen as students pass through school. Success is needed to keep students' achievement at individually appropriate levels. Success will eliminate most underachievement. If low-achieving students experience success and enter the "rich-get-richer" cycle, their achievement can exceed our current expectations for them. Also, since Matthew effects in reading are mutually enhancing with other cognitive skill areas, students' potential for achievement will actually increase.

The concept of Matthew effects comes from the Gospel according to Saint Matthew. It is the lesson derived from the parable of the gold talents: "For whosoever hath, to him shall be given, and he shall have more abundance: but whosoever hath not, from him shall be taken away even that he hath" (XIII:12).

"For unto everyone that hath shall be given, and he shall have abundance: but from him that hath not shall be taken away even that which he hath" (XXV:29).

We in education should be obligated to make certain that all children both have and be given the success in the abundance mentioned in the Gospel according to Matthew. Success for most low-achieving and disadvantaged students must be provided. It must be measured and monitored and planned for in their curriculum. Success for these students is not something they can consciously provide for themselves. It is not something that can be attained merely by changing our expectations. With our current assessment methods and curricular structures, these students neither have nor receive success. They are forced into the "poor-get-poorer" cycle by our lock-step system. We make them curriculum casualties.

The notion of success itself can be grossly misinterpreted. It can be confused with the handing out of trophies, plaques, and ribbons, or with A's, stars, or smiley faces. Success must be definable, observable, and measurable. It must be the central focus of our assessment procedures. Our assessment system should be success-based. The definition of success and the procedures for making sure a student experiences it are straightforward. This is true even though it is not widely known. Success-based assessment requires an active rather than passive relationship between measurement procedure and curriculum. Since it is curriculum-based, it makes the curriculum itself the assessment base. So, if a student's performance, while engaging in curricular activities, falls outside the success standard, the curriculum (or test) is adjusted to help the student's performance meet the success standard. This is the complete opposite of what is done in conventional measurement. Success-based measurement requires that the test (curriculum) be changed in order to produce the desired scores. With conventional assessment used for the purpose of giving grades, student performance is evaluated against one curricular level of difficulty, i.e. the same twenty-word spelling list for the whole class. With success-based assessment, the number of words on the list of spelling words given to each member of the class varies. The number of words is varied to reach the point for each student at which they demonstrate mastery, 90–100 percent accuracy.

We must take our definition of success from the observation of students who are succeeding and achieving very well. Fundamentally, success means that one is able to accomplish a task. All constituents of the task are performed correctly and the task is successfully completed. In learning, tasks must be performed correctly. Learning something is accomplished only if it is completed correctly a sufficient number of times to commit it to long-term memory. A primary component of success-based assessment is that it leads to success-based instruction. The metric leads to adjusting the curricular load so that each student is given tasks that can be accomplished correctly.

In learning to read, a new word must be correctly identified a sufficient number of times to make it familiar and instantly recognizable. In arithmetic instruction, the correct answer for each subtraction fact must be identified correctly a sufficient number of times so that the answer is produced automatically. In math activities like long division, the sequence of procedures must be performed correctly with sufficient repetition so that the correct procedures are performed automatically when division is called for.

Concept formation is fundamental to learning, but repetition, or practice, is also. Repetition or practice has two functions. First, it is used to maintain the newly introduced in short-term memory and then to create memory traces with more permanence in long-term memory.

Practice is needed to learn almost anything. Some people learn very quickly. They may need a relatively small amount of practice. This is especially true if the task to be mastered is in an area of their talent or aptitude. Less practice may also be needed for mastery if there is "transfer of learning" from a previously mastered task.

On the opposite end of the learning continuum are those students who require a great deal of practice or repetition for mastery. This includes students with limited talent or aptitude in the area of the task to be mastered and students who have limited number or fund of skills from which to transfer learning. Thus, the need for repetition is an individual matter, and there is a wide distribution of need in every classroom.

The element of success in repetition is, unfortunately, often overlooked. Teachers are often heard to say things like, "He's been over it a thousand times and he still can't do it," or "He's gone over it again and again, but he only gets it right half the time." These statements show that the role success needs to play in repetition is not considered.

We must remember that each repetition is only an effective repetition if a student gets the practice item correct. If the student gets the practice item wrong in the same way each time, it will be a learned error. If items get random or inconsistent responses, inconsistency in response will persist; the repetition accounts for nothing except lost time. A repetition is only a real, or countable, repetition if the student gets it right. An unfamiliar printed word needs to be associated with the familiar spoken word, either by decoding or by telling. Each arithmetic fact must be connected with its correct answer. The number of times a practice item is presented in a text, on a worksheet, or on a flash card does not count. It is only the number of correct answers to each repetition that counts.

The number of wrong and uncorrected answers will actually detract from the learning process. Students must succeed and show evidence of success at each step in drill and practice. Ultimately, it is only perfect practice that makes perfect.

The question may be raised, "If a student gets everything right, what is the challenge?" The answer to this question requires that a distinction be made between busywork and instructional level work. With instructional level schoolwork, new items, in appropriate numbers, are being introduced. These new items will need some level of practice to process them from short-term to more permanent memory storage. On the other hand, busywork is simply giving students work that has already been mastered. It is already in permanent storage. This kind of work is given simply to occupy time. It is unfortunately what can happen to many of the higher-achieving students held in each grade of the lock-step curriculum.

Doing appropriate instructional level work is challenging. This is so even though the level of accuracy or scores indicate success and high performance. However, the challenge should never exceed a student's ability to demonstrate these high performance levels. Much of the focus of educational assessment should be directed to observing and monitoring student performance on routine school activities to insure that these appropriate instructional levels are being maintained.

Low-achieving students are challenged far too much. They should be challenged at the same level as their high-achieving peers. If this is done, the work will proceed but at different rates. Maximum benefits to students accrue only when performance is very high. The indicators of performance should be in the same band for both high- and low-achieving students.

The amount of curriculum covered will be different, but it will be far greater than would otherwise be the case. When the performance scores are the same for all groups, Matthew effects will benefit low-achieving students also.

Determining the Instructional Level

How is the appropriate difficulty level determined? What is the appropriate difficulty level?

Basically, the appropriate instructional level must: (a) permit the student to engage in successful learning and, thus, avoid failure and frustration; and (b) advance a student along the curriculum.

More detail concerning the measurement of the instructional levels will be presented in a later chapter, but for the moment, a briefer description will suffice.

As a model for identifying or determining the instructional level in reading, the authors recommend what might be considered a classic. This is the model presented by Emmett Betts (1946) for the measurement and placement of student in reading material. Betts presents the criteria for measuring the student skill level and equating the student skill level with the different placement levels. He identifies and describes the independent, instructional and frustration levels.

The *independent level* is identified or described by Betts as the reading difficulty level at which fewer than 2 percent of the words encountered are words unfamiliar to the student and can be read by the student with at least 90 percent comprehension. It is anticipated the student will not need assistance to cope with reading material at this difficulty level. The student will independently be able to decode most of the unfamiliar words and comprehend the material well enough to grasp the main idea.

Providing reading material of this difficulty level, the independent level, is important for:

a. developing mastery, fluency and independence in reading.
   b. experiencing a high level of success which is necessary for reading to become an enjoyable activity and one in which the student will choose to do recreationally.

The *instructional level* is identified by Betts as the reading difficulty level at which approximately 2–4 percent of the words encountered are unfamiliar words and the student can read with at least 75 percent comprehension. When the student is presented with material with this difficulty, it is anticipated that the student may need assistance in identifying and comprehending some of the more advanced vocabulary. Also, the student may need to be prepared for reading the materials by discussing or explaining concepts or background information in order to comprehend the content.

When reading material of this difficulty level, the student is likely to need some preparation or assistance, such as:

   a. identifying and comprehending the more advanced or unfamiliar vocabulary.
   b. providing prerequisite concepts or background information necessary for comprehending the content.
   c. comprehending the writing style, intent or purpose of the writer.

The *frustration level* is identified as the reading difficulty at which the number of unfamiliar words exceeds 4 percent and/or comprehension drops below 75 percent. When reading material of this difficulty level is presented, the student is likely to:

   a. need more preparation and assistance than the teacher has time to provide.
   b. find the material too demanding and tire quickly.
   c. experience failure and become frustrated.

Betts's guidelines listed above should be used to directly assess the instructional appropriateness. However, in some instances a student will be able to read material of a familiar content area well above his or her usual reading level. This is because the student has the necessary (1) background of experiences and knowledge, (2) vocabulary mastery, (3) confidence, and (4) motivation and interest in reading such content area material. For example, a student with only fifth grade reading skills with a strong interest and background of experiences in auto mechanics may be able to read and comprehend the high school auto mechanics textbook. This student's comprehension may be much, much better than a student with tenth grade reading skills and no background or interest in auto mechanics.

Thus, the appropriateness of reading material has to be judged by checking student performance specifically in it. The student's achievement score and the reading level of a text should only be used as a general guideline and not applied rigidly or without exception.

There are other factors which may be considered such as cognitive ability, confidence and frustration tolerance level of the student. For example, the student with lower cognitive ability, a lack of confidence and a low frustration tolerance may need material of a slightly lower difficulty than recommended in the Betts model.

Somewhat different guidelines should be used in instructional activities in areas other than reading. This is especially true for presenting items such as new spelling words, math facts or a procedure requiring a sequence of tasks. Such instructional activities pose the question of "How many new items can be introduced, held in short-term memory, and then practiced to mastery?" Miller (1956) and Simon (1974) suggest a range of items that can be remembered. Simon's range of 3 to 7 items is more conservative than Miller's 5 to 9. Some students can concentrate on a few new items; others can manage more. Our experience suggests that low-achieving students will require numbers at the low end of Simon's range.

Ultimately, the number of new items or processes introduced is determined by checking a student's performance with the number of unknowns being varied. Ninety to 100 percent accuracy is desirable for practice activities. Remember, it is not profitable to practice errors. An accuracy range of 70 to 80 percent will be sufficiently comfortable to keep most students engaged and feeling reasonably successful. However, an accuracy range of 70 to 80 percent will be sufficiently comfortable to keep most students engaged and feeling reasonably successful. However, an accuracy range of 70 to 80 percent allows for a lot of opportunity to practice errors. Thus, student practice of material of this difficulty level is recommended only when guided practice can be provided and immediate corrective feedback is available. Independent practice should be reserved for material on which the student has demonstrated an accuracy of at least 80 percent.

Success and the ability to complete a task are strong, extremely motivating factors. Both of these reinforcing factors are the products of providing materials and content at the appropriate instructional levels.

Appropriate instructional level work permits students to engage in learning. Appropriate task difficulty permits students to engage in an activity and reinforces their willingness and ability to remain on task. Numerous studies validate the higher correlation between on-task time and achievement.

The more time students spend engaged in learning, the less time they spend off task. Off-task time results when tasks are too difficult. Students can't remain engaged in tasks that are too difficult. They might simply stare at the work, do it incorrectly, daydream or engage in disruptive behavior. Time the teacher may have to devote to dealing with off-task behavior can be far better spent in developing and providing instruction at the appropriate level.

Good work habits, good attitudes toward schoolwork and an adequate self-concept develop only if students are given work that they can become engaged in successfully. Schoolwork that is too difficult teaches students poor work habits, poor attitudes toward schoolwork, and avoidance of it. Schools that provide frustration level work to large percentages of their students are not viewed positively by those students.

To attain a high level of success and avoid both student and teacher frustration and failure, the teacher should strive to present instructional activities at a level in which the student can become engaged in with a feeling of success.

Entry Levels

The primary goal of assessment should be to prevent failure. This goal is achieved by matching the student's readiness level with the corresponding skill level. Matching the student's entry level into the curriculum with the student's readiness level is crucial to optimize the likelihood of success and avoid failure. Failure should not be permitted to occur when a student's readiness skills are not aligned with his or her grade placement in the lock-step curriculum.

A common practice is to presuppose the lock-step curriculum is an appropriate given and to assume students have the readiness level or prerequisite skills required to succeed in the curriculum. For students lacking this required readiness level or the prerequisites, failure is almost certain. The failure in not being able to do the work is usually followed by a failing letter grade. Too frequently the focus of this assessment is attempting to find out what is wrong with the student. In essence, we require students to fail and then assume something is wrong with them rather than in the system. Assessment should precede and so prevent failure.

Evaluate the Initial Placement and Monitor Progress

Curriculum-based assessment is used to determine the most appropriate entry level or placement in the curriculum. However, such data is not infallible, so the initial entry level or placement should always be considered tentative.

The student's performance should be monitored and evaluated after the initial placement has been made. The best method of evaluating the initial placement and monitoring progress is usually informal observations and assessments based on the student's daily performance. Student success rate in completing daily assignments should indicate satisfactory progress or an adjustment should be made. If informal observations and assessments suggest the initial placement is too low and not challenging, advance the student to a higher level in the curriculum.

It is indeed unfortunate that our current system requires student failure to be our first assessment procedure. It is also unfortunate that the second stage of assessment is the attempt to find out what is wrong with the student who is failing. We require students to fail and then we assume something is wrong with them rather than with the system which permits failure. Such failure can be prevented by conducting a curriculum-based assessment which yields data needed to identify the skill level in the curriculum which is compatible with the student readiness and skill level. Decisions can then be made as to what entry level into the curriculum will permit the optimal opportunity for assuring success and avoiding failure.

When students transfer from a different school system or begin studying new subject areas, assessment information should be used to protect them from failure and to insure that they succeed. Tests made from the scope and sequence of skills on the schools' curriculum (curriculum-based tests) and some achievement test information can be used to judge if students are able to move into new subject areas or at what levels the students have entry or readiness skills. All entry or placement decisions should be based on finding a position on the curriculum where the students are likely to succeed. Currently, our first assessment procedure is, unfortunately, failure itself; failing work and failing grades are the first assessment procedure we use. From this point, subsequent assessment effort may be directed to the failing student. However, the assessment effort will be directed to finding what is wrong with the student or what the student's deficiencies are.

Failure should be prevented. The first place to use tests to head off failure is in kindergarten. Readiness tests can be used effectively to determine which students are at risk for failing in first grade. More will be said about readiness tests in a later chapter, but for the moment a brief description will do. Readiness tests are usually norm-referenced with validity determined by how well they predict later school performance. They have been criticized for their inability to predict accurately specific levels of achievement in later grades. However, they are quite accurate in predicting which students will fail due to school-related abilities. Also, kindergarten teachers' informal assessment is likely to be accurate in determining which of their students are not mature enough to succeed in first grade. Information from these teachers and from readiness tests should be acted upon. There is no reason to send immature children on to stressful failure experiences. We have the misguided notion that children must move along with their chronological age peers through the lock-step grades. Kindergarten should be an enriching, open-ended experience from which children move with the skills necessary to succeed. This should be accomplished without regard to chronological age.

Grades give an inappropriate purpose to assessment. They give absolutely no specific information about where a student is on a curricular sequence. Altogether too much assessment effort is devoted to giving grades. This effort should be devoted instead to avoiding failure, insuring success, and actually measuring progress.

If assessment is used in this useful manner, then standard grading practices would not be possible. Maintenance of performance in success ranges does not permit a distribution of grades.

Chapter 3

TYPES OF TESTS

The results derived from educational testing are frequently numerical data or numerical descriptions. Interpreting or understanding the meaning of this numerical data may require an understanding of rather complicated concepts and formulas on which it is based or referenced. Sometimes the numerical data is based on the number right or wrong, a score or percentage. Sometimes the data is derived by comparing the results with results derived from others such as the norming population. Tests which are administered primarily for deriving such comparative or normative data are called norm-referenced tests.

The results derived from some tests may be used primarily to confirm if the student's performance or mastery level does or does *not* meet a predetermined or established criteria. The criteria on which performance or mastery may be based include factors such as time, accuracy, or level of difficulty. The primary purpose for administering the test is to determine if the student's performance or mastery level meets an established criteria rather than to derive normative data. Such tests are said to be criterion-referenced and, thus, called criterion-referenced tests.

There is another type of educational assessment that attends less to numerical results. Assessment procedures of this type provide more direct and substantive information than can be found in numerical indexes. They indicate the presence or extent of some specific skill or ability. The results of this measurement procedure is observable confirmation the student has the skill for performing a task in a lifelike situation. The observable confirmation may include the student using specified tools and materials found in a real-life situation such as on a job to produce a product of acceptable quality. The results are substantive. This is called performance or authentic assessment.

All three of these types of tests or measurements—normative, criterion, and performance or authentic—have necessary purposes or functions in education. The educator's task or responsibility is to select the type of test or assessment which best serves the purpose or function needed.

The goals for this chapter will be to provide insights regarding the:

1. overall purpose(s) of educational assessment,
2. various types of tests, including the three types briefly discussed above, and
3. selection of the right type of test or assessment procedure to meet specific purposes and needs.

Purposes of Educational Assessment

The primary purpose of educational assessment should be to insure success, success from the beginning, and success that is ongoing. Assessment should permit success by determining if a student is ready, has sufficient skill to begin instruction, or is able to move to the next instructional step. Assessment should be used to monitor the instructional process to make certain that an appropriate match is being maintained between student ability and instructional activity.

In most cases using this model, success results. When it does not, achievement falls below a student's learning potential. Assessment should be used to determine or identify the cause(s) for the lack of success and progress and appropriate steps taken to remediate the problem.

Finally, assessment should be used to evaluate the instructional process. Is instruction effective? Are the proposed curricular outcomes being achieved? The types of tests described in this chapter include those that may be used to serve these purposes. As each type is discussed, we will relate how they may be used to serve the purposes that we have proposed.

Norm-Referenced Tests

Teachers have traditionally used tests to measure the outcomes of a course of instruction. Teachers compose their own tests for assessing student mastery of the skills and knowledge presented or to be mastered. These teacher-made tests are useful in providing specific information regarding student mastery and what remediation or reteaching needs to be done.

These teacher-made tests do not allow for comparison of student performance within the class. However, they do allow for comparisons of performances with a larger referent and identified group of individuals, usually referred to as the norming population. To make comparisons beyond the class, the teacher must use a standardized test commonly referred to in the past as a norm-referenced test.

The items for a standardized test are carefully constructed and evaluated. Precise administration procedures to be followed during the administration of the test are developed. The test is then administered to a representative sampling of the target population for which the test was developed—a designated grade level, age grouping, etc. Numerical data (raw scores such as the number of items correct) is collected from administering the test to the sampling of the target populations. Appropriate norming statistical procedures are then applied to the numerical data collected to derive norms or standard scores for the target population. The norms or standard scores more commonly derived include percentiles, stanines, and grade equivalents. These norms or standard scores can then be used for comparing the performance of an individual or groups—classes, schools, districts, states, etc.—with the performance of the target population used for standardization or norming.

Achievement tests standardized in this manner are frequently used in an attempt to measure the effectiveness of instruction. Using such tests to measure the effectiveness of instruction can have several fallacies. One major and common fallacy in using standardized tests as a measurement of the effectiveness of instruction is the lack of an adequate sampling between the goals of the curriculum and the test items. If a standardized achievement test is to be used for this purpose, the test items must have a representative sampling from the skills and knowledge to be taught at each of the grade levels to be tested. Otherwise, the test cannot be a valid measurement of the effectiveness of instruction.

Standardized achievement tests have been criticized for the lack of correspondence between test items and specific curricula (Jenkins and Pany, 1978; Shriner and Salvia, 1988). The major reason for this lack of correspondence is that adopted curricula materials, such as basal texts, are frequently published by different publishers than the standardized achievement test adopted by the school system. Content validity is the most important quality an achievement test can have. The content validity of an achievement test will vary according to how well its items correspond to the items that comprise any given curriculum. Consequently, the content validity of an achievement test is really only determined by comparing its items with the scope and sequence of curricular items.

The curricula of the various school systems in the country have some common content at most grade levels and it is this content that test constructors attempt to sample when they devise an achievement test. Further, the content that they use generally must lend itself to being tested in the multiple-choice format. This usually means four answers to choose from. The less-than-best or clearly wrong answers are called distractors.

This test format has many advantages. Tests with this format are efficiently scored and are readily statistically analyzed. Scoring the tests is done reliably. However, the test format itself further limits the content validity of such tests. Few instructional activities dealing with any curriculum item bears much resemblance to this test format. Content-valid measurement requires that items be as similar as possible to the actual learning activity.

Despite problems with content validity, standardized achievement tests do measure achievement in a more general, not a specific, way quite well. These tests are not particularly helpful in guiding the specifics of instruction for individual students. They can do a good job of showing whether or not and how much achievement is occurring in individuals and in groups. They cannot tell specifically what to do to improve instruction. They simply do not provide enough specific information. The scores tell almost nothing in this respect, and even an examination of the actual performance in the test booklet or answer sheets can tell very little. There are just too few items representing each subject and each grade level to be of much use. For help in instruction, teachers need more detailed criterion or curriculum-referenced tests that reveal details.

Items selected for norm-referenced tests typically go through the following process. Pools of items that are common to each subject area at various grade levels are assembled. These items are tried out on large samples of students. Items are selected from this process by their difficulty level in this standardization sample. The difficulty of the item, the percentage of students failing it, is considered as is its ability to discriminate between students whose scores on the total test are in the top 27 percent and those whose scores are in the bottom 27 percent. Items are selected that represent a hierarchy of difficulty levels in fairly even steps, from 1 to 99 percent failing. Also, the items must discriminate between the high scores and the low scores on the test.

The items with these qualities are assembled into the completed test. The number of items correct, the raw scores, are made into a frequency distribution for the standardization sample. The norms for the test are based on this distribution of scores. Standard scores, percentiles, and grade equivalents are derived from this distribution.

Though the content validity of most standardized achievement tests is not sufficient for helping guide instruction, they are adequate for evaluating achievement in a more general way. Great effort is made to select items that are common to various curricula and curricular materials for each subject. The normative process insures that the items selected for each level reflect things being learned at each grade level in the standardization population. The number of items that are used to measure achievement in each subject at each level of difficulty is quite small, but the number is sufficient to make a fairly good estimate of the amount learned.

Standardized readiness tests are more difficult to find items for. Content validity is not as obvious an element in the selection of items that are used to predict how well some skill will later be acquired. For example, a content-valid reading test contains words and passages of increasing difficulty which must actually be read. The thing being measured is the important part of the test. However, in the case of a reading readiness test it is necessary to assess the aptitude for acquiring reading skill without using the skill itself.

The items selected are thought to be prerequisite reading skills or simple skills that seem to be a part of reading. One of the best predictors that is included on most reading readiness tests is recognizing individual letters of the alphabet (Hargis, 1982). The items selected seldom predict later reading skill acquisition with much precision. The skills measured may indicate only helpful abilities that are useful in acquiring the skill of which they are an assumed component.

Readiness tests have been criticized for this lack of precision. They do not predict specific levels of later achievement with accuracy. They can't predict which students will receive A's or B's or C's in a classroom after instruction has proceeded for some time. However, this is really a trivial point, though much is usually made of it. The criticism masks the important function of readiness tests. We should be primarily concerned with protecting students from failure. It seems startlingly inhumane to start six-year-old children in first grade classrooms if the odds are great that they will fail. This in fact happens every year in first grade classrooms. Three or four children are failing and that many more are meeting with only marginal success (Glasser, 1971; Hargis, 1987). Readiness tests with adequate predictive validity (about .50 or better) will identify, with quite good accuracy, the performance level below which students are likely to fail when instruction starts (Hargis, 1982).

Readiness tests will indicate many of the children who are at risk for failure because of lack of readiness. Enrichment readiness activities or simply more maturational time before formal instruction begins will help these students. However, there are children who are at risk for failure because of health factors or some problem in their environment. Information on these other factors that place children at risk for failure may not be revealed in readiness test performance. Problems in these areas account for the number of students who fail without being identified by readiness tests—about 15 percent of those that are at risk for failure.

In sum, norm-referenced or standardized tests have a prominent role to play in educational assessment, but the roles we recommend are not always those of current practice. Norm-referenced tests can be used to evaluate the effect of instruction. They can be used to prevent failure and help insure success. They often are used, however, simply to label or classify students for the purpose of fitting them in some slot or other in the lock-step structure of our schools.

The most controversial use of standardized achievement tests has been in the evaluation of teaching. This should not be such a controversial issue. Achievement tests are used to test the effect of program changes and of alternate methods and materials. Teachers are certainly as important variables in classrooms as a new set of instructional reading materials. With achievement tests that are reliable, have adequate content validity, and are sensitive enough for the particular students being tested, starting and finishing achievement should be measured routinely. Positive changes in achievement should be expected. Certainly, if there is no change, or negative change (as is the case in some unfortunate circumstances), the teachers' performance should be questioned. Something is wrong and should be remedied immediately. If the teachers are at fault, they should be assisted to improve or reform. If this does not work, then the teachers should be dismissed.

Criterion-Referenced Tests

Criterion-referenced tests measure performance or levels of knowledge on specific content. Instead of producing scores that simply rank students or compare them to others, the scores are expressed in terms of the knowledge or skills achieved. The substance and focus of attention of criterion-referenced assessment is what skills and knowledge are to be mastered by the student. Consequently, the item selection for criterion-referenced tests is usually different than for norm-referenced tests.

Items developed for criterion-referenced assessment not only represent the domain to be assessed but a specific skill level in a hierarchy of skills within the domain should be comprised of the domain being measured. The content validity of criterion-referenced tests is the primary consideration. When criterion-referenced tests are constructed, the content of the particular domain is converted into test items. Each item is intended to answer the questions: Does the respondent understand this item? Or, Can the respondent perform this task? For example, "Has the student mastered addition facts have sums of a designated quantity?" or "Can the student perform addition computations requiring designated skills and concepts?" In this way, progress toward mastery of a domain of skills or knowledge can be assessed.

Criterion-referenced tests emerged to focus measurement on specific content. Criterion-referenced instruments were developed that sampled the content of specific domains of achievement or skill. The tests are designed to tell where instruction should begin. This means that the test should represent adequately the skills that comprise the domain. Also, if there is an order to the acquisition of the skill, the items should be ordered in this hierarchical sequence. This test organization facilitates finding where instruction should begin and what skills remain to be presented.

Criterion-referenced tests have been prepared to fill voids in curricular offerings. This has been especially true in special education and early childhood education. This was and is the primary reason for the development of the Brigance® series of tests. Criterion-referenced tests actually represent the curricular outline for the domain they test. Criterion-referenced tests often become the curriculum for the teachers who use them. The tests may only sample the skills, but they point the way to preparing detailed daily instructional activities that support and fill out the scope of objectives. The tests provide the summative evaluation that tells the teacher whether or not the student has learned the content of instruction. The formative, or ongoing, assessment is the informal monitoring of the progress being made on the daily activities that are to lead to mastery of the objectives.

Criterion-referenced tests are typically adopted to serve curricular and instructional needs. They tell what to teach and what to teach next for individual students. Criterion-referenced tests imply that instruction must be individualized and that progress will be individually gauged.

The domain or curricular area is the basis for selecting test items. The items are determined by analyzing the domain or task to be taught. This task analysis forms the basis for both the curricular objectives and the test items.

In the task analysis, the items are ordered in terms of prerequisite skills. Skill areas that are basic to subsequent ones are placed first in the instructional sequence. Skills that are constituents of more complex ones are also ordered accordingly. Criterion-referenced tests are structured with the same order in mind. These procedures are quite different than those used to select and prepare norm-referenced test items. The discriminating qualities of the items are not typically considered. With criterion-referenced tests, the important factor or quality is the extent to which the test assesses the subskill tasks that make up the domain or criterion and mastery of the task itself.

The notion of mastery and the measurement of this abstraction has proved problematic. The problem really has been in attempting to establish scores or cutoff points on test performance that would suggest when a skill or domain has been mastered. Whether 70, 80, or 90 percent correct of the items measuring some criterion suggests mastery does not seem to us a relevant or useful issue. Correct items should simply point to what has been learned and incorrect items to the unlearned. In short, tests should be primarily an aid in guiding instruction.

The content validity of criterion-referenced tests can be questioned, as there is subjectivity in item selection. The items selected are based on an analysis of components or subskills that make up a domain or skill area. Such selection can lead to controversy, as there is not always agreement as to what subskills lead to mastery of a domain. Reading specialists or authorities, for example, frequently disagree as to what subskills students should master to become effective readers. Consequently, items selected for criterion-referenced assessment will vary among these specialists or authorities.

Math subskills are viewed in various ways also. Consequently, the "task analysis" may be a consensus-building process. For example, item selection for a criterion-referenced arithmetic test could include the following procedures: The test constructor will collect the popular commercially prepared arithmetic programs, the arithmetic curriculum guides for states and large school systems, and the arithmetic portions of widely used achievement tests. From this assembled body of data, the constructor will look for commonality of occurrence and placement of individual items and skills. They also consider the most usual in the format of presentation. The items for the test are selected and ordered by their frequency and most usual placement.

Criterion-referenced reading tests can be constructed in a similar manner as can criterion-referenced tests in any other subject area where curricular material and achievement tests are available.

In domains where there is limited material available to review or analyze to identify commonalities, the test developer must assemble the items for the test from an analysis of the skill to be measured. The task analysis requires direct observation of the skills in question. For example, the test constructor developing a test for assessing the skills needed for independent living must divide this large domain into subdomains— shopping skills, personal care, housekeeping, etc. Then some of these subdomains such as shopping will need to be divided into units such as shopping for food, clothing, household items, insurance, etc. These assessment units may be developed from instructional units, *or* instructional units can be from assessments. Regardless of which is developed first, it is crucial there be a high degree of correlation or corresponded between the two.

Curriculum-Referenced Testing

In recent years the concept of a third type of testing, curriculum-based assessment (CBA), has begun to emerge (Hargis, 1987; Tucker, 1985). When discussing this concept, some writers may use the terms *curriculum-based measurement* (CBM) (Shinn, 1989) or *curriculum-reference testing* (CRT) interchangeably (Hargis, 1982). This new concept (curriculum-based assessment) has emerged primarily because of the low degree of content validity which frequently exists between the content, scope or sequence of specific curricula and commercially available norm-referenced and criterion-referenced tests.

The basic idea of this concept is that the test items or assessment tasks should be drawn directly from the specific curriculum. In effect, curriculum activities and tasks can be used as the assessment. This concept affords a great deal of integration between instruction and assessment and has been called the ultimate in teaching the test (Tucker, 1985). The formative and summative tests are directly drawn from the curriculum being used. This concept has emerged and gained recognition, as it assures a high degree of correlation (content validity) between assessment and the instructional program. With this high degree of correlation, the results obtained from this type of an assessment are easily translated into remediation strategies and instructional objectives.

Beyond this common point, CBM and CBA differ markedly (Hargis, in press). The advocates of CBM depart from those who are proponents of CBA on two principle points. The first is that CBM is a norm-referenced system. The test items are drawn from the curriculum and then normative information is determined by administering the tests in specific locales and using these data.

A basic assumption underlying CBM is that learning problems are defined as performance discrepancies. Significant performance discrepancies are shown by a small number of students who don't meet the "reasonable" expectations set in general education programs for their grade and age peers. These expectations and discrepancies from them require the development of empirical norms. Learning problems are defined as a measured normative difference from reasonable expectations for a student's grade and age peers. The purpose of education or special education is to close the gap between actual performance and expected performance as determined for age and grade peers.

We disagree in principle on this point. Norms established around our lock-step curricular and school organization distort the normal variation in learning and achievement rates that we should expect. Trying to force children to fit standards and expectations based on the lock-step curriculum organization of our schools is what has caused our problems already. This system produces the curriculum casualties we have alluded to elsewhere.

We argue that curricula should be fitted to students, not the reverse. This fitting of the curriculum to the student was a primary reason for the development of criterion-referenced testing and later for the development of curriculum-based assessment. This issue is a fundamental rift between CBM and CBA. Students should be permitted to work at the highest step on the curriculum where they can perform as comfortably as their high-achieving peers. This should be done without regard to expectations based on lock-step norms.

With CBM, the measurement of performance discrepancies and the development of local norms become central activities. The end result of measurement becomes simple numerical description. It isolates assessment from instructional activity.

With CBA procedures, assessment is not isolated from the instructional process. Assessment is used for immediate action and feedback. If a student's performance is observed to fall below appropriate instructional levels, the time to act is at that moment.

The primary objective of CBA is success. Measurement that is an intrinsic part of instruction is used to insure that instructional levels are always maintained. CBM does not consider instructional levels or success. The number of words read correctly per minute, the number of letters spelled correctly in a word, or correct numerical responses are passively charted and graphed. Rate of progress or lack thereof are examined at summative points and only then will the course of instructional activity be changed if progress appears unsatisfactory. The difficulty of a task and the failure and frustration of the student attempting to engage in it is only a matter to be charted in CBM. In CBA, this problem would require immediate action to insure the student could engage and succeed in any routine instructional activity.

With CBM, routine performance will be left to vary. It will be duly noted graphically. The instructional level metrics are not part of data collection. With CBA, the variation in performance levels are restricted by design to instructional success levels.

Items for CBM tests and monitoring probes are drawn from the instructional material being used in the classroom. A routine monitoring measure for reading might be reading a list of words containing the phonics skill being taught at the time. A summative test would be reading orally a passage from the basal reader being used to check fluency. In the routine testing the number of words read correctly over a specific duration are recorded and graphed to plot progress over time. With the oral reading test, the fluency rate per minute would be graphed each week over the school year.

In either of the above CBM procedures, identifying the instructional level is not a consideration. What is under consideration is the shape of the graph. Does the slope of the line indicate that there is an increase in the number of words correctly identified and is there an increase in fluency of oral reading? If after 10 or 12 weeks, there is little or no improvement, change in instructional method may be recommended. CBA's method of assessment is less formal and is a part of instructional activity. It is not intrusive. Routine assessment is the observation of the students engaging in instructional activity. If their performance falls below the instructional level standard or if the task is too hard to persist in without stress and frustration, the activity and materials are changed or modified to produce successful instructional level engagement.

Summative assessment at extended periods is used to chart progress along the curriculum hierarchy. Students are not permitted to fail or do poorly. The metric is used to adjust and match material and activity to the students in order to achieve the desired performance levels.

CBM measures are not concerned with measuring performance while engaged in learning activities. Students could be having to cope with work so difficult it is producing frustration and failure. Measurement is done by means of probes, the results of which are used to graph change. Decisions about taking action only occur after extended periods of time and inspection of the graphs, during which time students may well be failing.

CBA is a continually active assessment process that is intrinsic to instruction. CBM is a passive and intrusive measurement procedure which is isolated from instruction.

Performance and Authentic Assessment

Most norm-referenced tests and many criterion-referenced tests are paper-and-pencil, multiple-choice tests. The multiple-choice format is ubiquitous. True/false tests are common but probably more so to teacher-prepared tests.

Ease and reliability of scoring are primary considerations for these test formats. Certainly, when specialist teachers are preparing their own exams, they will have to administer around 150 tests at a time. Certainly ease and reliability of scoring have to be major factors. The grading practices we use require that there be a number of test scores in the record book each grading period. The demands on teacher time becomes oppressive if more than a minute or so per test is required for scoring and recording.

Grades are the objective of most classroom tests. The detailed substance of what is learned is not a main consideration. These tests are assumed to be adequate enough samples to suggest how many of the instructional objectives have been learned, but their primary purpose is grading.

Complaints about classroom tests and achievement tests focus on the lack of substantive information about what is actually being learned. Further, the test format, multiple-choice and other objective types, is subject to much criticism.

Even with their criticism, both of these assessment concepts will continue to exist. Compared to some of the newer and emerging assessment concepts, these types of tests allow for a great deal of ease of administration and scoring. The ease of administration and scoring cause these types of assessment to have a great deal of appeal to the teacher confronted with the task of administering and scoring tests for large groups such as 150 high school students in five class periods. Basically, in many situations both concepts serve their intended purpose when used correctly.

The greatest shortcoming both norm-referenced assessment and criterion-referenced assessment is that they are limited to the pencil-and-paper format. Justifiably, they have been severely criticized by personnel involved in programs in which the assessment of skills does not lend itself to the pencil-and-paper format. This includes programs in which a crucial part of the assessment is "Can the student apply knowledge and perform the taught skills in context, in the real world?"

The skills being tested are usually out of context. They don't represent the real application of a skill. Performance assessment has been used to measure skills more directly. Because of the criticisms of conventional assessment procedures, performance assessment is being recommended as an alternative.

Primarily due to the shortcomings of conventional assessment methods and procedures, and the need to assess skills in context rather than "on paper," the concept of performance assessment has emerged. As one would expect, this assessment concept has gained very favorable acceptance in areas such as vocational trades or crafts which have never found pencil-and-paper tests to be adequate.

With performance assessment, the student is evaluated based on an assigned project or a product produced as part of the class work. For example, samples of the apprentice welders' work are evaluated at each stage. Visual examinations of quality are used, and stress tests are applied to see if a weld's strength is adequate. The skills of the apprentice bricklayer may be assessed based on workmanship qualities such as levelness of the bricks, the plum of the wall, the correct spacing between the bricks, the adhesiveness of the mortar to the brick, etc. The assessment of secretarial student's skills may be based on completing a product such as a letter by using a word processing program in a designated amount of time which meets prescribed standards such as being free of typing and spelling errors. These concrete measures with obvious content validity are examples of performance testing. This same level of content validity is sought for academic assessment.

Performance assessment has always been used in music. Instrumental and voice performances are judged directly. It would be hard to imagine how it could be done otherwise. Debate contests and merit badge projects in scouting are other examples where performance assessment is used. The term *authentic assessment* will frequently be used in place of or interchangeably with *performance assessment.* It is usually used to indicate that the performance being assessed is related to an authentic real-world skill.

The evaluation of written composition is the most likely to be considered authentic assessment. However, the need to directly evaluate writing was the case before the terms *authentic* or *performance assessment* came into use. The methods for grading or evaluating written composition has evolved with attempts to produce more reliable scoring procedures. Reliability has been noted as a significant problem in evaluating written language, since Starch and Elliot's (1912) classic study showed how unreliable were the judgments of English teachers in grading the same composition.

In other curricular areas, samples and examples of student activities can be selected. They can be evaluated by an individual or a group of evaluators trained in using a standard so as to make more reliable judgments. Experiments, projects, and portfolios of work are subjected to this evaluation.

Making the format of classroom instruction less like that of a standardized test was another reason for changing test formats. Curriculum and instructional activities tend to be test-driven. Consequently, content and format of tests should resemble the desired authentic outcomes in the real world. If instruction follows this course, the skills learned will be more likely to transfer and apply to larger domains.

Criterion-references tests have more focus on subskills or domain constituents. Critics feel they cause teachers to overemphasize fragmented subskill and drill activities. One of the potential problems with performance assessment is that it can reduce attention to detail that needs an ordered instructional progression. A compromise will probably emerge.

From our view, the principle problem with performance tests is in the way the results are used. If they are simply used as another way to give grades or determine relative performance rather than to determine progress and to provide success level instruction, then we object.

Scoring standards and rubrics are used to make scoring reliable, but it is consistency in producing scores and grades that is sought. A score or letter grade is evidence that the test is used normatively and passively. If the tests are used to and do produce a distribution of scores or grades, it means they are not being used to guide instruction so individually appropriate progress can be made. Performance assessment may more validly represent the domain, but if it is used for comparisons and grading, its benefits are lost.

Performance assessment can have beneficial effects on the mode of instructional activity. Instructional activity should begin to be more authentic and interesting, less like an objective test. However, as long as the tests are used normatively rather than substantively, they will be little better than current methods. The purpose of the test needs to emphasize what has been learned and what to do next to produce success and achievement on individual bases.

Informal Tests

Informal tests are typically the teacher-made tests that are routinely given as a basis for awarding grades to students. Even if used primarily for this purpose, informal assessment should be done for the purpose of guiding instruction.

With the teacher being aware of the content which has been presented or taught, a representative sampling of test items can be selected from instructional activities or generated. Thus, there can and should be a high degree of construct validity.

If the tests are used only for grading, teachers will use some scoring standard on a scale such as: 95–100 is an A, 90–95 is a B, etc. Sometimes teachers will work out grades based on a normal distribution.

Informal tests in some subjects such as spelling and basic math can be scored very objectively. The same is not true for informal tests for some skill areas. Reliability in scoring informal tests becomes more difficult to achieve as subjectivity increases.

Scoring writing samples with a fair degree of reliability has been and continues to be a challenge. The Ayres Handwriting Scale of 1912 was one of the earliest attempts to offer a solution to this problem. It provided teachers with a set of handwriting specimens with which to compare student samples. The score was based on the quality of the student's sample relative to the standard.

Various scoring criteria and standards have been presented in more recent years for evaluating written composition. Some of these criteria and standards have been effective in increasing scoring reliability regarding intelligibility, grammar, and coherence. However, elegance and creativity are still very much subjective and reliability among raters continues to be low. Nevertheless, students are frequently graded on these abstract qualities.

Informal tests should be used primarily to guide instruction, not to give grades. Whether or not a teacher can reliably use various scoring criteria, the net result of assessment will usually be a letter or score. Neither of these indexes do more than compare students to other students or to a standard. The abstraction of the index itself provides no useful idea of what the student needs to be doing or learning next.

The focus of informal assessment should be on gaining substantive information, not normative indexes. For example, a letter grade of A on a math assignment or written composition does not suggest where a student is on the learning continuum of either subject. Does the grade mean that the student has managed to master the threshold skills required to match the scale or scoring criteria, or does it only indicate that the test sampled skills the student has already learned? It is possible that the test is only sampling skills that are well below the student's learning threshold?

Perhaps the students should be better engaged in composing sonnets rather than in writing friendly letters, or working on differential equations rather than on multiplication tables. The point is that informal tests should help point to what is learned and where to go next. The information should be substantive, not normative. Actually, this should be true for most educational measurement.

The baseline or basal level of performance should be identified. This is the level in any curriculum area where instruction should begin. It is the point at which the student's readiness is sufficient to begin work on the next, more difficult task. The basal level is comprised of a foundation of skills and abilities that are mastered. Much assessment activity should be devoted to finding these basal or baseline skills. They mark not only the point at which instruction should begin but the current achievement level of the students. The achievement level will be reported by the specifics of what has been learned rather than by a normative index.

Another important, but often neglected, feature of establishing a baseline is that it requires focusing on skills learned rather than on deficiencies. The baseline or threshold tells what abilities that comprise a domain of skills have been mastered. Appropriate instructional level activities occur at the edge of this baseline.

When the focus of assessment is on deficiencies and weaknesses (as it so often is), the quality and usefulness of the assessment information degenerates. Testing for grades speeds the degenerative process along. The purpose of testing is only for the production of scores so that a grade can be determined. A distribution of scores is desirable so that a distribution of grades can be assigned. Errors are even desirable. One level of test is administered to induce errors and produce a distribution.

Useful informal measurement requires that different levels of tests and measures be used to probe the variety of skill levels that exist in most classrooms. The variety of skill levels would be demonstrated by the distribution of scores produced when one grade level test is given. Proper, informal assessment maintains individualized instruction. If there are many different instructional ability levels in a classroom, that means there must be that many levels of informal assessment. Assessment levels change with instructional levels.

An informal test given to a class to produce a range of scores for grades does nothing in the way of finding and maintaining baseline instructional levels. The errors on such tests do not help in finding a skill threshold.

Curriculum-referenced tests are used to find the entry-level point where instruction should begin. The informal measurement that continues is to make sure that the instructional level is maintained. It should be an integral and unintrusive part of all ongoing instruction.

Any instructional activity in which students are engaged should be thought of as an informal test. Is the activity of appropriate difficulty? Can the student remain successfully engaged in it? Is the performance level high enough that the student has little opportunity to practice errors? These are the kinds of questions to be answered when observing students engaged in ongoing instructional activities. There will be more discussion regarding this kind of assessment in a later chapter.

Construct-Referenced Tests

Constructs are theoretical notions about psychological processes. Prominent among such constructs are intelligence, creativity, attitude, motivation, aptitude, dominance, even reading comprehension.

Some would argue that with a lack of agreement as to how constructs such as creativity should be defined, they cannot be measured. The existence of the construct some of these tests purport to measure is evidenced only by more concrete skills or behaviors. Thus, such tests tend to create controversy. Such controversy frequently leads to discussions such as, "To what degree should scores on intelligence tests be associated or equated with academic achievement potential?" or "To what degree can novel and inventive behaviors and performances be predicted by scores on a test purporting to measure creativity?"

Tests purporting to measure these various constructs usually include the construct as part of the test title. The test's title may be the only evidence given as to what the test is purporting to measure. The definition of the construct used in developing the test is compared to the items it contains. This is subjective. Better evidence of the existence or validity of the construct are usually found in areas such as aptitude or readiness. Perhaps the major reason for a higher degree of validity usually associated with these constructs is that the items included in these tests tend to be more representative of the domain in question. The tests then are made up of the behavior or skill in question. However, results derived from tests measuring these constructs (readiness and aptitude) should always be evaluated in light of other student data available—health, disabilities, culture, interest, motivation, etc.

Recently, meta-cognition and learning strategies have emerged. Meta-cognition refers to the awareness and control of one's thought processes, such as the planned development and use of a sequence of learning strategies to enhance attention, knowledge acquisition, retention, or performance (Wittrock, 1991). Meta-cognition seems to be a construct developed to replace another older construct that has a tarnished image, namely, intelligence. Doubtless, much energy will be devoted to developing tests to measure, and treatment programs to ameliorate, deficits in them. It is a good idea to maintain a certain skepticism about constructs that attempt to cite problems in a student without considering the curricular structure the student is required to fit.

Some constructs, and tests made to measure them, exist with a fair degree of acceptance with very little creditable evidence to support them. In some cases, they persist even after evidence suggesting that their validity is most questionable has been accumulated. Even if the construct appears to exist and to be measurable with some validity, there may still be a lack of evidence of significance regarding how they can be useful in improving instructional programs.

Several theoretical constructs have been developed and promoted to account for learning problems and educational deficiencies. Some of these constructs have caused a tendency to identify or explain the basis or cause for a student's learning problem(s) as residing within the student. Several such constructs have emerged: hyperactive, attention deficit disorder, processing deficits, motivation for the unmotivated, etc. The existence of some of these conditions within some students is unquestioned by the authors. However, the basis or possible cause(s) for the existence of such learning problems should be considered as environmental (extrinsic) prior to focusing on and accepting a cause or diagnosis having an intrinsic basis or cause.

Too frequently, there is a reluctance to accept the primary cause(s) for a learning problems as being environmental (extrinsic) and not intrinsic. Numerous environmental (extrinsic) factors have been validated as the major or contributing causes for such learning problems. These environmental factors may include:

- a poor learning environment (including the student being out of synchronization with the lock-step curriculum)
- poor health (mental or physical)
- allergies (food and environmental)
- poor diet

Environmental factors should be considered, evaluated and ruled out as possible causes prior to attempting to identify, and accept, an intrinsic cause as the basis for a learning problem.

Chapter 4

RELIABILITY AND VALIDITY

A quality a test should have is that of giving consistent results. The degree to which a test can be relied on to give consistent results when administered to the same or similar groups is referred to as its reliability. The reliability of a test is the degree or extent to which the results of the test are stable and can be trusted.

A valid test measures the skill or behavior which it claims or purports to measure. However, the ability of a test to measure what it claims or purports to measure is not absolute but varies by degrees. The degree to which it measures what it purports to measure is referred to as its validity. The most important factor in the selection of a test is that it have an acceptable degree of validity. When selecting a test, these two proven qualities—reliability and validity—are crucial. There is a very close relationship, but they are not the same thing. A reliable test gives consistent results. Consequently, a valid test is necessarily reliable. The reverse is not, however, necessarily true. It is possible that a test can be consistent in yielding results (reliability) but still not be a valid measure what it claims or purports to measure (validity).

Tests can consistently produce quite similar results or rank students in the same order when repeatedly administered. However, tests can be consistent in scoring or ranking without satisfactorily measuring the behaviors they were intended to measure.

Reliability and validity are occasionally confused because they are often reported in terms of a correlation coefficient. In the case of reliability, the test is being correlated with itself or parts of itself. In the case of validity, the test is being correlated with other similar measures. The index is the same, but the meaning is really different.

Mathematically minded test constructors (or statisticians) often go to great extremes in their attempts to prove the technical adequacy (statistical data) of tests. They are very concerned with a few mathematical indexes related to reliability and to validity.

Indexes such as validity and reliability are crucial in the construction of some types of tests such as norm-referenced tests. However, when developing other types of tests such as curriculum-based tests, the emphasis or focus should be on having a high correlation between the test and curriculum rather than statistical documentation. If proving "technical adequacy" becomes the major concern or emphasis in the development of such a test, it may negatively affect the desired outcome—that of having a high correlation between the test and the curriculum.

Reliability

The key word regarding test reliability is *consistency*. Can the test be trusted to yield consistent results when administered several times? This reliability may be established or proven by using different methods or procedures.

There are several types of test reliability, with each type having its own purpose. The type of test reliability the test developer seeks to achieve and confirm usually depends on the type of test being developed. Different methods or procedures are used in confirming each type of test reliability. The purposes of three major types of test reliability and the methods or procedures used to establish or confirm each type are explained below.

Test-Retest Reliability

The main purpose of this type of test reliability is to confirm the test can be trusted to yield consistent results when administered several times. One method of establishing test-retest reliability is to administer the test to the same student or group of students more than once. If the scores or results obtained from each administration are consistent (do not fluctuate significantly), test-retest reliability is established or proven.

This reliability is usually determined by correlation. Consistency over time is determined by correlating the scores on the first administration of a test to a group of students with the scores obtained on a second administration of the test to the same group of students at a later date. The assumption here is that if the items in the test are reliable, they will produce the same response through repeated administration. If responses fluctuate, the items may be ambiguous, thus producing inconsistent responses. Also, inconsistent responses can be caused by variable administration procedures or testing condition. Problems with determining reliability in this manner include the possibility of "practice effects."

Familiarity with test items may improve scores. Another problem can occur when the time between administration of the test permits growth or achievement on the traits or skills being measured.

An extension of this method is to develop two forms of the test: Form A and Form B. Both forms are then administered to the same group of students. If the scores or results from both forms are consistent (scores on each form are basically the same), equivalent forms reliability is established or proven.

The equivalence of the two forms is determined by the correlation coefficient produced when both forms are given to a group of students. This correlation is an estimate of the test's reliability. High reliability suggests that both forms of the test are valid measures of the same trait. If there is lower reliability, it may be that the items that comprise the tests are not sampling the domain's content equivalently, and hence, neither form may be confidently considered a valid measure of the domain in question. Again, this form of reliability speaks directly to content validity.

Internal Reliability

The main purpose of this type of test reliability is to confirm that the items included in the test are consistent in being of the same level of difficulty. One method of establishing internal reliability is to administer the test to a group of students. Then score the odd-numbered and even-numbered items separately. If the scores obtained from scoring the odd-numbered items and the even-numbered items separately are consistent (basically the same), internal reliability is established or proven. This type of reliability, internal reliability, is sometimes referred to as "split-half" reliability.

The internal consistency of a test can be determined through a single administration of the test. The test can be divided into two equivalent halves and then scored as if they were independent tests. Then the two sets of scores are correlated. If the test is made up of items that are carefully sequenced in difficulty, the test can simply be divided by even and odd items. Then the scores from the two halves are correlated. In both of the above cases, a high correlation (a coefficient approaching 1) indicates that the test is internally consistent and the items are measuring the same domain or subject area.

Tests that show low internal consistency may not be good measures of the domain being measured. In other words, the items may not be a sufficiently broad or accurate sample of the skills that make up the domain being measured. Each of the halves of the test is considered an independent sample of items from the total number that make up the domain being measured.

If the two samples don't correlate too well with each other, then the total test sample is unlikely to be well related to the total domain that the test is intended to measure. This type of reliability also speaks directly to the content validity of the test. Good internal consistency does not mean a test is content valid, but it is a necessary condition for it to be so.

The length of a test affects its reliability. The more items a test contains, the more reliable it can be. Calculating reliability from halves of tests reduces test length. The reliability coefficients will consequently be lower. Each of the methods of calculating reliability can produce different reliability coefficients as well.

Interrater Reliability

Tests made up of multiple-choice or true/false items are objectively scored. Scoring student responses to such items requires little or no subjective judgment of the scorer. Thus, when these tests are scored by several different individuals, the scores given by different scorers are consistent.

The same is not true of tests comprised of essay-type items. Scoring student responses to such items may require a great deal of subjective judgment on the part of the scorers or raters. Thus, when several raters score the written composition of the same student, the score given by the different raters may vary and be very inconsistent. If the scores given by the different raters are inconsistent, the test will be subject to criticism as have poor interrater reliability.

A classical study or example is the research work reported by Starch and Elliot (1912) regarding the lack of reliability between English teachers scoring English papers. They had two compositions evaluated by 142 English teachers. They found a 47-point range of scores on a 100-point scale. One paper received 15 percent failing scores and 12 percent above 90.

The main purpose of this type of test reliability is to confirm that the test can be scored by different raters and yield consistent results. To accomplish this purpose, the test developer must construct the test so that the scores granted by different raters are as consistent as possible. If a test is constructed so there is a high degree of consistency in the scoring granted by different raters, the test is considered as having good interrater reliability.

Subjectivity can be understood in grading written composition, but the same subjectivity can also be found in mathematics test when items require more complex problem solving than can be evaluated by a multiple-choice test item. Here again, Starch and Elliot (1913), in a classic study of reliability of scoring, found the range of scores on geometry paper were even greater than they found on the English papers!

Standardized tests typically avoid subjectivity by using primarily multiple-choice and true/false items. These tests are standardized with very specific directions for administration and scoring. Tests with this structure reduce the amount of fluctuation in scores that can be produced by individual examiners. In many instances the tests are scored by computer.

The greatest problem with reliability is with the many informal classroom tests that are used for grading purposes. There are many different variables that influence reliability when teacher-made tests are used for grading (Hargis, 1990). Grades don't mean the same thing from one teacher to the next, though they teach the same subject at the same grade level. Grades don't mean the same thing from one school system to the next. The standards may be different or the standards may be imprecise. Further, it is difficult to control the quality of test items when they are constantly being created for informal testing.

Standardized tests containing subjectively scored parts such as written composition require carefully structured scoring standards. Adherence to these standards permits similar scores to be produced among multiple scorers or raters. The more judgments an examiner must make in scoring a test, the more precisely the scoring procedure should be structured. Strict adherence to these procedures will be required to assure the reliability of scoring. Many individually administered tests require a considerable amount of judgment in scoring or rating. The administration procedures and the scoring procedures are spelled out in detail. These procedures must be followed in order that the results can be relied on to represent the tests' purposes.

Error of Measurement

The reliability coefficient permits the calculation of the standard error of measurement (SEM). The standard error of measurement indicates how much a test score is likely to vary if it is given repeatedly to the same person. A test's SEM provides an indication of the accuracy of a score obtained on a test. For example, if a test has a standard error of measurement of 4, the scores obtained on the test will likely stay within a range of plus or minus 4 points two out of three times (about 68%) on repeated administrations of the test. The SEM provides an index of confidence that can be used to judge the accuracy of the scores obtained on a test.

The SEM is calculated by using the standard deviation of the distribution of scores obtained on the test (on norm-referenced tests it will be calculated from scores obtained on the standardization population). The reliability coefficient of the test is calculated by checking the internal consistency or consistency over time. The standard deviation of the test's scores and the reliability coefficient are used to calculate the SEM. The higher a test's reliability (a decimal fraction approaching 1), the smaller the SEM will be. Smaller SEM's mean that we can expect that a score obtained on a test is fairly close to a true score.

The standard error of measurement should be used to temper or qualify the confidence we have in test scores. A test score is more properly viewed as a range of possible scores. Tests are only relatively small samples of traits or behaviors. There are many ways that error can occur to affect test reliability. The quality of the test items influences the amount of error. The number of items (test length) affects the amount of possible error, conditions under which the test is taken, qualification of the examiner, as well as the physical and emotional state of the examinee. All can influence the reliability of a score. The error of measurement should be viewed as a good confidence boundary for a score only insofar as the other factors are approaching the ideal.

Criterion- and Curriculum-Referenced Reliability

The difficulty of test items is important to determining reliability by correlational method. Test items need to be discriminating. They need to separate or differentiate between examinees of lower skill levels from those of higher skill levels. Items that are all answered correctly or that are all missed do not contribute to a test's reliability. Items that contribute most to correlational reliability are in the intermediate range of difficulty, that is, missed by about 30 percent up to about 90 percent of the examinees.

Reliability that is correlationally determined requires variation in scores. Item difficulty or discriminability is important in producing a range of scores. In the case of criterion-referenced test reliability, the production of a range of scores is not or should not be a consideration. Variation in the total score of curriculum-referenced tests is of less interest than what skills or behaviors exist or don't exist. Most standardized tests and most classroom tests are used to compare, rank, label, classify or grade students. Total test scores are used for this purpose. A range of scores is required. The score itself becomes the be-all and end-all of test administration.

With curriculum-referenced tests, the focus changes to what specifically a student knows or doesn't know. The test items themselves become the focus of attention. If the test is hierarchically sequenced, a basal skill level is sought. This is the important level at which instruction should start. It is the entry level on the curricular path.

The basal level is the highest level at which the student performs successfully. The level at which items are missed indicates those that constitute what should be the focus of instruction or remediation. Reliability with curriculum-referenced tests refers to the confidence that can be placed in a test to show the mastery or achievement of skill or knowledge. Since mastery of specific content is of primary interest, the number of items measuring it must be sufficiently large to show that the skill has been mastered and that correct responses were not just chance responses.

We have found, for example, that three consecutive correct responses in learning simple math facts or sight words is good evidence that they will be retained long term. On criterion or curriculum-referenced tests, the mastery of specific, discrete skills can be measured by two or three items. Mastery is in evidence if all items are correct. If the content is embedded in multiple-choice items or true/false items, then chance becomes more of a problem. Two good four-response, multiple-choice items are equivalent to at least four true/false items. Again, one miss in any group suggests no mastery of content.

Reliability in curriculum-referenced tests also can depend on test length. This time it is the number of items measuring each area of the domain in question. There needs to be a sufficient number of items to give reliable evidence of what specifically has been learned. Mastery along a continuum of curricular objectives marks both current achievement level and the point from which subsequent instruction should start.

Reliability based on scores in CBA is not of much relevance when the scores themselves tell nothing about the specifics of what has been learned or not learned. This specific information is what is of interest.

One condition that is necessary to conventional reliability is actually antithetical to CBA. This is the requirement that there be heterogeneity in a group of scores (a wide range of scores) in order for the test to show high reliability through correlational methods. The scoring procedures that are of interest in CBA (the type advocated by Tucker, 1985; Gickling, 1985; and Hargis, 1987) are those that indicate a good curricular-to-student match has been made. These scores are those that indicate the students are engaged in learning. They are the instructional level scores that are to be maintained in all instructional activities. They are in a fairly narrow band in most curricular domains. The instructional level scores were described earlier and will be reviewed in later chapters, also. However, to briefly review, in reading, and in activities that require reading, students should understand 96 percent of the vocabulary and maintain comprehension of at least 75 percent. In problem-solving, drill, and seatwork activities in general, performance should be maintained above the 75 percent correct level.

These guidelines are used to monitor ongoing instructional activity. All instructional activity in which a student engages is a test to be evaluated. Instructional activity itself becomes a test, but it is a test to be manipulated to achieve the desired scores. Conventional reliability notions are turned upside down. Scores are to be maintained at the same level by design, but in order to do this the test must be altered to fit the individual student. For example, if a student were given an assignment in math and only 50 percent of the problems were completed correctly, the teacher would adjust the difficulty level of the assignment so that the student's performance would reach into the instructional level range.

Mastery

Some authors concerned with criterion or curriculum-referenced assessment are concerned about mastery decisions (Ebel and Frisbie, 1991). This usually means establishing a cutoff point where the decision can be made from test results. Will it be 90, 80, or 60 percent correct? Will it be a specific point on a scale? These points are arbitrarily established, and they are used for grading and classification. They focus attention on a score rather than on the content of what has been learned.

With CBA, mastery decisions are made when students perform a task successfully with consistency. Mastery is a function of the reliability of responses. When students are able to perform a task correctly on a consistent basis, then it has been learned. When a student has demonstrated the same level of performance on several occasions in a more subjective area of learning, those samples are evidence of mastery.

We have found that for many subject areas, mastery can be reasonably assumed if the student performs a task correctly on three consecutive occasions. For example, if a student can correctly identify a word on three consecutive occasions in spaced practice, the student is likely to be able to recognize the word instantly from then on (Hargis, Terhaar-Yonkers, Reed, and Williams, 1989). Reliability in the measurement of mastery is dependent upon consistency of performance. It is an important measure in CBA, because it tells when a curricular item can be added to the fund or stock of skills and can be used as the basis for further learning. It also tells when new items can be safely introduced as replacements and then instruction can reliably proceed at appropriate instructional levels. Mastery decisions should be made as a part of instructional activity. They are not well made from the results on single tests.

Validity

Validity refers to how well a test measures what it purports or claims to measure. There are several types of test validity, with each type having its own purpose. The type of test validity the test developer seeks to achieve and confirm usually depends on the type of test being developed. A different method or procedure is used in confirming each type of test validity. Three major types of test validity are discussed below. The purpose of each type of test validity and the method or procedure used to establish or confirm each type are explained.

Content Validity

The purpose of content validity is to have confirmation the test measures the domain (objectives, curriculum content or subject area) that it purports to measure. It provides answers to questions such as "How well or to what degree do the test items sample or represent the skills and concepts which need to be assessed?"

In order to insure content validity, a test must be made up of items that compose the skills to be measured. This means the test items must have a high correlation with the curriculum goals and objectives. Ideally, these curriculum goals and objectives are represented by test items in terms of their importance or priority.

In fairness to the student and to carrying this idea one step farther, the test items should be a representative sampling of the skills and concepts presented or emphasized in the instructional program. For example, there should be more test items assessing skills and concepts which were given priority and emphasized for a week and very fewer test items assessing skills and concepts which was briefly dealt with during part of a class period.

The need for a high degree of content validity lead to the development of the curriculum-referenced tests. These tests usually provide the highest level of content validity. This assumes the test items unambiguously represent the curricular goals, the instructional objectives and what takes place in the instructional environment. Therefore, most content-valid tests in education are tests that are made up of the items that are being taught. Good content-valid tests in education are the ultimate form of teaching to the test (Tucker, 1985).

As discussed previously, the lack of content validity of many standardized achievement tests has been the primary reason for the development of the movement towards criterion-referenced and curriculum-referenced testing. These problems prompted the development of criterion-referenced tests in both academic and life-skill domains that could serve both purposes at the same time. Criterion-referenced tests that serve as both curriculum guide and achievement tests have become popular in special education.

Some states have undertaken the development of basic skills curricula and have developed tests that measure progress toward the attainment of those specific curricular objectives. As states developed minimum competency or proficiency tests, many teachers of low-achieving and disadvantaged students adopted the test content as a part of their curriculum. There is an obvious intuitive desire to see content validity in testing. If certain content is important enough to test, then it should be taught.

There should be an intimate relationship between curriculum and test. Moreover, to insure that a test is content valid, it should be composed of items that resemble the manner in which the content was taught. With curriculum-based assessment, most of the measurement is done by direct observation of the student engaged in the activity during routine daily work. The assessment procedure authentically assesses performance in this way.

A test's content validity is determined in one of three ways. First, a test can be selected by comparing the test's items to the curriculum in use to see how well the items correspond in both type and location to curricular objectives. The second method is to prepare the test by systematically sampling curricular items representing every stage of the scope and sequence of skills and then preparing test items for them. The latter procedure may be the only way content validity can be assured when a specialized curriculum is prepared or adopted. The third method is to adopt a comprehensive criterion-referenced test as the curriculum guide. More detailed objectives will be needed to fill out the scope and sequence of skills for teaching, but the basic content of the curriculum will then be assuredly sampled by the test.

There is another way content validity of a test may be considered. If a test contains items that are not a part of what is being taught or are poorly represented on a curriculum, test results may reflect on the validity of the curriculum. Test results would suggest revision of the curriculum, if the test suggests deficiencies in desired skill areas.

In this use of a test, the content validity of the test is considered independently of the curriculum. The test is used to sample desired skill domains, and the curriculum itself will be evaluated through student performance on the test. Tests measuring desired subject or skill domains may be used as the basis or driving force to alter or adopt a new curriculum when the curriculum itself may lack validity.

The validity of the content of a test or of a curriculum is determined by the judgment of school boards and school personnel. The developers of standardized tests have their own notions about what constitutes content validity. If the vision of what constitutes valid content by any of these groups varies, there will probably be a problem with content-valid measurement. There needs to be an intimate relationship between a test and its curriculum or a curriculum and its tests.

Criterion-Related Validity

The purpose of criterion-related validity is to determine how well the results derived from two or more assessments instruments correlate. It answers the question of "How well do the results derived from assessment X (the criterion test) compare or equate with assessment Y?"

Determining criterion-related validity can be a very useful procedure to use when considering changes in assessment such as changing from one test to another. For example, a teacher might need to make a decision regarding the selection of reading material to be used with 150 ninth grade students in his five social studies classes. To help make this decision in previous years, the teacher administered Reading Test X which takes 40 minutes to administer and each test takes approximately 1 minute to score.

A new test, Reading Test Y, which can be administered in 20 minutes and each test scored in less than 30 seconds, has been recommended as a replacement for Reading Test X. However, the principal has expressed his concern that the 20-minute test (Test Y) will not be as effective as the 40-minute test (Test X) for making these decisions as to what reading material should be used. What evidence can be presented to the principal as proof Test Y (the 20-minute test) should be considered as a viable replacement for Test X (the 40-minute test)?

Establishing or confirming Test Y yields essentially the same results as Test X and can be used as evidence Test Y is a viable replacement for Test X. Test X is the criterion by which Test Y will be compared or evaluated. In order to establish or confirm this criterion-related validity, both tests are administered to the same group of students. Then the scores from both tests can be correlated by computing a correlation coefficient between the scores for each test. An acceptable correlation coefficient is supporting evidence Test Y can be considered as a viable replacement for Test X.

In essence, the merits by which Test Y is being judged or evaluated is how well the scores from it compare with the scores from Test X, the criterion test.

However, this correlational evidence of validity does not provide evidence as to how effective either test is in making the decision regarding the selection of the reading material. If the criterion test, Test X, had been proven to be valid assessment for making this decision and a high correlation coefficient existed between Test X and Y, there is reason to believe Test Y would be a valid assessment for making this decision.

Curriculum wise, a more practical method of determining criterion-related validity may be that of comparing the teacher's evaluation of student performance with results derived from a test. For example, the math supervisor knows that numerous research studies have concluded the evaluation of student performance by the observant and competent teacher is a valid assessment method. The supervisor believes Mrs. Blake to be a very observant and competent math teacher. How can the supervisor determine which standardized math achievement test, X or Y, has the most criterion-related validity?

This can be determined by administering both tests to Mrs. Blake's math students at the end of the year and comparing the test scores with Mrs. Blake's evaluation or ranking of the performance of the students. In other words, the Blake's evaluation or ranking of the performance of her students becomes the criterion by which Test X and Test Y are evaluated. If Test X has a higher correlation with the teacher's evaluation or ranking than Test Y, it is the one with more criterion-related validity.

The same results would also suggest Test X is the test with greater content validity, as the results suggest it is the test which correlates best with the instruction or content presented by Mrs. Blake.

Obviously, the correlational evidence of this criterion-related validity and content validity is dependent on the validity of the criterion measure, the letter grades or scores granted by Mrs. Blake. The same results may be referred to as concurrent validity, in that the evidence is collected at the same time. Current skill levels were measured using teacher evaluation and two tests that purport to assess the same set of skills.

Predictive Validity

Predictive validity serves as the basis or evidence for predicting what level of success a student or person can be expected to achieve in a given program (environment) based on present performance or data.

The predictive validity of a test is the accuracy with which the results from the test can be used to predict what degree of success a person can be expected to make in a specific school program or career—kindergarten class, high school, graduate school, electronics, etc. The predictive validity of a test is the correlation between the test's scores and a criterion performance measure. Predictive validity is determined by correlating a test's results with results from an acceptable measure of performance at a later date. For example, a reading readiness test is given at the end of the kindergarten year and a standardized achievement test is given to the same students at the end of the first grade year. The results of the readiness test are correlated with scores on the reading portion of the achievement test to see how well the readiness test (the predictor) correlates with the reading achievement measure (the criterion).

The ability of the readiness test to predict success or failure in beginning reading activities is of obvious interest. A test is useful if such inferences about performance can be drawn from the scores.

Perfect predictive validity would be indicated by a correlation coefficient of +1.00. This is a perfect positive correlation. A perfect negative correlation is indicated by a coefficient of −1.00. No relationship is indicated by a zero. Most tests that are used to make judgments about readiness and later success or failure have rather modest ranges of predictive validity coefficients, about .40 to .60. These may seem like rather low correlation coefficients. Actually, we are usually only concerned about predicting general, not specific performance levels. We should be concerned about avoiding failure, not predicting specific scores or grade points on the criterion performance.

Tests with proven predictive validity are frequently used when making placement decisions at all educational levels—first grade reading program, high school algebra or medical school. Vocational recommendations and decisions regarding career choices are frequently based on results from tests having predictive validity for specific careers.

Tests with predictive validity can, if judiciously used, result in more successful placements by helping to avoid misplacements likely to result in failure. Scores in the marginal or questionable range can help to identify students who may need remedial instruction or preparatory studies prior to program placement. Such scores can also identify students who may need special help, such as tutorial services, in order improve their chances of success if admitted to a program.

Construct Validity

Constructs are theoretical characteristics or traits. They are abstract notions such as creativity, higher-order thinking skills, problem-solving ability, motivation, and learning style. Evidence for construct validity is difficult to gain directly. Unlike content validity which is achieved by sampling directly from the behaviors or skills to be measured, construct validity must be established by indirect means. The items selected to measure a construct are embedded in other activities or skill areas. Problem-solving or reasoning ability is often measured using sequences of arithmetic operations. Estimates of the extent of its existence may use verbal directions of varying complexity which require reading or verbal ability. Word games, puzzles, mazes, analogies, block designs, vocabulary measures, and still more, are used as vehicles for measuring constructs. Ultimately, construct validity is determined, or claimed, by using criterion-related validity procedures. The test of the supposed construct will be related to individuals who apparently exhibit the trait in question. Individuals who demonstrate the trait will perform well on the test and those with less of it will do correspondingly poorer.

New tests of the trait have their results correlated with other tests that are accepted measures of the construct. Significant correlation would suggest construct validity through this criterion-related procedure.

Constructs are difficult to define precisely. However, they are often related to characteristics of unquestionable significance, and the existence of a good many of them is not denied. Higher-order thinking skills, problem-solving and reasoning ability are currently of interest, and it is believed that they are not adequately considered in either curriculum content or achievement measures.

Undeniably, it would seem wonderful if our schools could teach students to be more intelligent, reason more efficiently, solve problems more effectively, and think more creatively. However, these are all constructs. They are to varying degrees abstract and difficult to define. Nevertheless, to establish construct validity, the construct must be defined clearly enough in some way to make test items that conform to the definition. The tests that purport to measure most constructs are sometimes ambiguous and of questionable validity (Ebel and Frisbie, 1991). Does the task of completing a figure analogy measure intelligence? Does the ability to list unconventional uses for a brick measure creativity?

Do constructs so difficult to define and test items related to such constructs in rather questionable ways make valid curriculum content? The answer is no, and when such curricula are prepared to teach the constructs, the results in terms of improved performance are usually equivocal at best. Granted, there usually will be changes in performance on the test used to measure the construct in the first place, but that improved performance will be the result of teaching to that test. Transfer of the skill or trait to improved performance in actual subject areas is disappointingly absent. Constructs are often viewed as magic bullets which if fired at academic deficiencies will solve all problems. Many constructs have been proposed as explanations of variation in the academic performance of students. Treatment programs have been prepared to remedy deficiencies measured with tests of these constructs. Improved performance on these construct-referenced tests after such treatment programs is often used as the evidence of the validity of such tests and their constructs. This is really not sufficient evidence for construct validity. Improved academic achievement would be the primary evidence of the significance of trying to teach the construct in question and hence the construct validity of the test. Such transfer of skills seldom is witnessed.

The development of many construct-referenced tests is really the result of inadequacies in our educational system, not inadequacies in students on these traits. Our lock-step system of curricular and measurement organization encourages these misplaced efforts, and to paraphrase Justice Holmes: The obvious is what needs to be understood, less so the arcane.

Arithmetic achievement is improved by using content-valid tests that directs teaching at appropriate instructional levels to insure a student's success and continuous progress. No thinking skills program or learning style alteration will make a student conform to an inappropriate placement in a lock-step curriculum.

Summary

We emphasize the importance of content validity. There must be an intrinsic relationship between what is taught and what is tested. We emphasize an added perspective on reliability: it is essential that all students do extremely well consistently. This means that for routine instructional activity, performance must be held in a narrow band that is indicative of success and engagement in learning. In other words, if scores can be given, they must be the same for all students. The instructional activities must be viewed as tests that are managed for individual students to produce these success level scores.

On achievement measures or tests of progress along the curriculum, we recommend that reliability be attained by preparing items that are not ambiguous and are appropriately placed in a curricular hierarchy.

We need specific evidence of what the students have learned more than we need normative scores. Instructional decisions are precisely made given what the students are able to do and what they can engage in doing next with the likelihood of success.

We need to consider reliability from the perspective of the position of the test or curricular item. Does it consistently appear in the same position in the hierarchy of difficulty? Is the item appropriately placed with respect to its readiness relationships with other skills?

We need to change our view about the desirability of a wide distribution of scores in order to establish the correlational forms of reliability. We need to want consistent homogeneity of scores around the success interval. Consistency of success should be an added hallmark of reliability.

Chapter 5

TESTS FOR INSTRUCTION: SUCCESS-BASED ASSESSMENT

Most teachers, if asked about their experiences with testing, would tend to describe the testing that goes on in their schools as intrusive, disruptive, irrelevant, or that it is a chore necessary for assigning grades. We agree with their feelings. Assessment should be so much a natural part of instruction that it is not even considered a separate activity, let alone an intrusive one.

Curriculum-based assessment should be conducted initially to determine the student's appropriate entry level into the curriculum. This assessment should provide answers to one or more of the following questions:

1. Does the student possess the prerequisite readiness and skills to assure success and avoid possible frustration and failure?
2. If the student does not possess the prerequisite readiness or skills, what special help or remedial instruction may be needed to compensate for any deficits?
3. Does the advanced skill level suggest advanced placement be considered in order to provide the challenge needed by the student?

There also needs to be a means of identifying problems that are interfering with learning that is attuned to the curriculum in use. Finally, the students themselves should have the means to be engaged in self-assessment to monitor their own progress without apprehension.

Entry Level

Level of instruction and grade level are the same in lock-step curriculum systems. Grade placement determines where instruction starts. The curriculum scope and sequence is assigned to each grade from kindergarten through the twelfth grade. Generally, students are assigned to a grade according to their chronological age. With their chronological age peers, the students are to partake of the curriculum offering according to their personal ability levels. The curriculum sequencing by grades produces the lock-step order. All students, regardless of ability level, must proceed through at the same pace from the same starting point. At the beginning levels, teachers may organize ability groups, usually three, to manage the wide range of ability levels. The instructional burden may be reduced for some, but three groups in no way approach the actual range of entry level skills and learning rates that normally occur at the primary levels. Occasionally, schools will use "transition" classes, which are an intermediate step between kindergarten and first grade, to hold students until they are a little more ready to join the lock-step march through the grade sequence.

Inevitably, when students are assigned to curricular slots, casualties occur. Variable students do not all fit rigidly proscribed slots in the lock-step. Curricular sequences cannot be assigned to grades and then students to the grades without casualties. Curricular sequences must exist unrestricted by lock-steps of grades. It must be lengthened or shortened in a way that does not cause casualties at one end and limit the achievement to below the potential of students at the other end.

Measurement in education should not focus on the consequences of fitting students to the lock-step curriculum. It should focus on placing individual students at appropriate places on any curricular sequence. This point, or entry level, has several defining characteristics. It is the instructional level, or point at which a student can engage in learning comfortably and successfully. It defines the basal or baseline skill level of the student. It defines the fund of skills upon which subsequent instruction can build. It marks the current level of functioning or achievement. It provides benchmark points from which achievement gains and accountability measures may be taken.

It should further be noted that substantive information rather than normative scores should be the result of assessment. Specific information, the details of what a student can do, is necessary information for defining an entry point where progress can occur successfully. To illustrate this point, consider the following experience:

A group of adolescent boys who were in a classroom for learning disabled in a junior high school were included in a reading research project. The project was intended to check certain behaviors while the students were engaged in reading. It was necessary to determine the current level of reading achievement for each of the students. All of the students had received the same standardized achievement tests at a recent date, and the grade-equivalent scores in reading on each student were identified so that reading material with the same readability levels could be matched with each of them.

The grade-equivalent scores for the boys ranged from about 1.5 to a little over 2.0. High interest, low readability materials were selected with the range of readability demonstrated by these students. The books were provided to them and an informal check was performed to see if the match had been satisfactory.

Each student was to read orally from the book provided to see if it was within the instructional level range described by Emmett Betts (1946). It became immediately apparent that we had not accomplished this. None of the boys was able to read even as much as half of the words encountered!

It became quite apparent that grade-equivalent indexes from the tests were not even approaching adequacy in identifying a specific entry level where reading activity could commence. It also became quite apparent that we needed to look for more specific and direct measure of reading ability if we were to find reading materials that the students could engage in.

It was through using actual reading instructional materials as informal reading tests that we found that the standardized tests were actually far less sensitive than this informal procedure. It subsequently became apparent through using this same informal procedure in checking the suitability of more material that we would have to find still more specific substantive measures if we were to find entry-level reading material that these boys could actually engage in reading independently. Since no reading material could be found in which any of the students could engage successfully, it was decided that such material, at the individual instructional reading levels of the students, would have to be composed for them. Since instructional reading material must be composed of at least 95 percent known words, an inventory of the words actually known by each of the students was undertaken. The inventory list was made up from the vocabulary that comprised each of the high interest, low readability books we had previously selected and tested for use with the students. The list of words from each book was administered as a sight word test to see which and how many of the words could be recognized.

The number of words each student knew from these lists would become the basis for composing and preparing instructional level reading material. Whatever fund of known words each student had would be used as foundation vocabulary, the 95 percent known words that would permit meaningful engagement in reading. The remaining percentage would be the unknown words taken from the same list. This was the plan. However, the number of sight words we found that each of the students actually could recognize was painfully small. The sight-word vocabularies for the boys ranged from about a dozen to something over forty words. After more than six years in school, the boys were still non-readers.

A dozen words, or even forty words, is a very constricted vocabulary for use in written composition, as we soon found. We did, however, manage to produce reading material in each case that was at an instructional level. With so few sight words, it required being very repetitive with those few. Literary impulses had to be checked. The preparation of instructional level material and insuring student success was paramount. The reading selections for students with the most restricted vocabularies were, of course, the most repetitive and had the most simple and constricted sentences. The material was carefully prepared in regard to format. There was no large print and the general format was acceptably age appropriate.

As it turned out, and as it has turned out on a very great many occasions since then, the students found nothing objectionable about the language restrictions. The ability to engage in and perform successfully is so surprising and reinforcing that the literary limitations seem immaterial.

This stage is only transitional until the fund of words is increased to the point at which 95 percent of the vocabulary has been mastered for the targeted reading material—basal reader, high interest-low readability book, tradebook, etc. At this mastery level the student enters the reading activity at an instructional level. Success has been formally planned and has been part of the activities at each step.

The details of assessment and instructional materials are tied together. The reading material to be used is the first part of the test. This provided insufficient detailed information to find an instructional level entry point. The next step was to identify, in detail, specifically what the students could do so that an instructional level entry could be achieved. The vocabulary list provided this information. The vocabulary lists became both the curriculum and the test. Specially prepared materials were required to help students learn, at an instructional rate, all of the targeted vocabulary. This is the vocabulary that the books were composed with and would need to be known in order to read at an instructional level.

These boys all had some limited reading ability. They had learned the basic concepts about print. They knew what words were and that words were comprised of letters. They recognized all of the letters, both upper and lower case, and they knew the left-to-right, top-to-bottom physical representation of printed language. If students are encountered who know no words and have not as yet acquired these basic concepts about printed language, then the assessment procedures and the curricular items must cover these readiness/entry levels.

These were the lessons learned from these testing and teaching experiences:

1. Standardized tests do not provide sufficient information to guide basic instructional activities.
2. The instructional material itself should be used as the primary assessment material.
3. It is most important to find those things that students are able to do. With the lowest-achieving students, this can require a detailed assessment search.
4. Testing should not be an after-the-fact activity, separated from instruction. Assessment should be a part of the activity. Is the activity too hard, too easy, or about right? If it is too hard, change it immediately. No educational benefits accrue from failure and frustration.
5. Only the actual curricular materials can ultimately be the measure of entry-level skills.
6. At the beginning reading levels, using grade-equivalent scores to select reading instructional material is too imprecise to be of much use.
7. Students should not be permitted to fall farther and farther behind their potential. Failure is the cause of this, but students do not willingly fail. Failure is imposed.
8. Non-achievement results from forcing students into curricular activities that are above their instructional/entry level.
9. The lock-step curriculum misdirects our assessment efforts. We look for causes of problems in students instead of a mismatch with student and curriculum level.

10. Students need protection from the lock-step organization of the schools.
11. Students need protection from grading practices which encourage lock-step organization and therefore produce poor performance.
12. Normative scores and letter grades do not provide specific enough information for guiding instruction.

Entry-level skills and abilities are those that students have mastered and can do consistently well. Mastery of a particular skill or curricular item is determined by how reliable the student's performance is on them. Generally speaking, for isolated skills or facts in math, reading, and spelling, the ability to perform the task on three consecutive, separate occasions is reliable evidence of mastery.

With written composition, written samples should show consistency at each level of sophistication. Some curricular areas such as written composition are made of a complex of skills that must be consolidated in their performance. Improved performance depends on identifying the component parts that most need improvement or most interferes with intelligibility. Within the context of the activity, those subcomponents with priority for improvement are attended to, and their mastery is demonstrated when they have reached the standard on a consistent basis each time the activity is performed.

Achievement and mastery must be measured by examining the details and subskills, attending to them, providing for sufficient practice on them with helpful feedback, and, finally, checking to see if they are consistently incorporated in the activity. Scores or grades draw our attention away from these details of instruction. Mastery and achievement are evident in the task's consistent performance with the subskill done according to the standard. Does the student consistently mark sentence boundaries with capital letters and periods after direct attention to this skill? Does the student regroup (borrow or carry) in multi-digit subtraction and addition problems?

Daily activities should be monitored for these changes in performance. The performance should not be monitored simply for scores and grades. These have no relevance to working with important curricular details.

Intrinsic Assessment

Throughout this book the importance of a "marriage" between assessment and instruction has been and will be stressed. Too frequently, assessment focuses on the product or outcome at the end of the instructional activity or period. Assessment should be part of the "process" as well as part of the "product." If evidence of performance is gathered at the end only, there may not be the awareness the program is ineffective and program changes are needed.

From The Instructional Level to Mastery

One major reason for integrating instruction and assessment is to keep the instruction at the appropriate skill level—the instructional level. Maintaining instruction at the appropriate skill level can be a challenge even for the most competent teacher. Continuous observations and assessment are crucial in achieving this challenge.

Perhaps the best guideline for achieving this challenge is "Can the student respond to or perform the tasks with 80 percent success?" However, 80 percent may not be appropriate for all students. Students with a low level of confidence and low frustration tolerance are likely to need more than 80 percent success. Students need to do well to learn well. If the material is too difficult, more guided practice and monitoring by the teacher is required.

Perhaps the best guideline for mastery is "Can the student perform the task independently and functionally at the 95 percent level or above?" Teacher judgment regarding fluency, automaticity, and consistency are also an important part of assessing master of some skills.

For some skills, the above guidelines are not appropriate or adequate for determining mastery. This includes skills for which transfer and application should be a crucial part of mastery. Transfer and application of skills cannot be assumed. For example, the student may demonstrate mastery of subtraction problems at the 95 percent level or above but fail miserably when required to apply the concepts in performing daily living skills such as making change in ordinary monetary transactions.

Authentic or performance-based assessment requires authentic or performance-based instruction. If transfer or application of a skill is a desired outcome of instruction, the activities that require application of the skill should be an intrinsic part of instructional activity.

There seems to be a prevailing notion that problem-solving or reasoning skills are discrete constructs or abilities. Following this is the view that these constructs might even be learned as separate subject matter. We hold the view, however, that skills of application and problem solving are most effectively learned in task- or subject-specific ways. The problems and applications of any subject area should be included as a part of the specific curricular area. Transfer of training of problem-solving skill should not be assumed.

Diagnostic Assessment

When students are learning less well than they should be able to learn, then the cause of the problem should be identified. It is unfortunate that our primary diagnostic procedure seems to be failure. Too frequently take no action until and unless students is a chronic failure. Most failure is the result of the improper fit of students to the lock-step curriculum. These curriculum casualties account for most school failures. However, there are a minority of failing students who have problems that interfere with learning. Consequently, when students do poorly in school the first diagnostic procedure should be to establish whether the problem results from the lock-step curriculum or from something in the students.

Vision and hearing screening are the first steps. The essential features of sensory assessment are outlined in Chapter 11. Students should be free of, or freed from, these difficulties before diagnostic assessment proceeds further.

The second step is to determine whether or not the lock-step curriculum is the cause of the learning problem. To do this requires the identification of the student's instructional levels. Instructional level material in which the student can engage and perform according to those standards is the necessary assessment material. Reading materials or instructional activities that require reading must be selected in which the student's comprehension reaches 75 percent or 90 percent. These represent the instructional level and the independent level, respectively. They should encounter fewer than 5 percent unknown words for the instructional level, and fewer than 2 percent unknown words for the independent level. For drill and computational practice activities, the students should be able to reach at least 75 percent accuracy. These steps in the assessment process are simply finding an appropriate entry level.

After this level has been established for the students who are being evaluated, then they are observed when they are engaging in this appropriate entry-level material.

If the students are able to engage in the activities, stay on task, and complete them, then there is no significant learning disability. Some caution should be taken in interpreting the results too quickly. Students who have experienced chronic failure can have developed disintegrative attitudes toward instructional activities that may take time to overcome. Students who are clearly avoiding engaging in the activity may need some extra time, even several days, before they come to realize that the material is not just another source of pain and frustration.

Usually the change in behavior becomes apparent even as the instructional levels are being identified. Another factor usually becomes quite apparent also. This is the discrepancy between what is found to be the students' instructional level and the level of difficulty that constitutes their regular schoolwork. The reason for their learning problem is usually apparent at this point: The students are simply not able to do the work assigned to their grade level.

Observation of student performance can begin after the student has been supplied with instructional material at an appropriate level of difficulty. If the students are also to engage in and complete the work, the curriculum mismatch is the culprit in the students' learning problems. If, on the other hand, the student cannot remain engaged and complete the work within reasonable time limits, the cause may reside in the student.

If students are easily distracted, these off-task behaviors may need specific attention. The instructional environment may need changing to encourage more attention and to remove distractions. The work itself may need to be apportioned in shorter segments. In short, there may be a "real" learning problem that may require specific adjustments in order to work around it.

Continued inability to engage in instructional level activity may be the result of factors other than some "real" learning disability. Nutritional problems (even hunger), allergies, neglect, abuse, and family disintegration are among the problems that can produce learning difficulties. Each will need to be considered as a cause. However, the curriculum must first be eliminated as a cause by finding an appropriate entry level and observing performance at that level. If the off-task behavior persists after sufficient opportunity to feel success, then other causes must be sought out. The instructional environment and the instructional format can be modified to eliminate distractions and encourage increased attention. Success itself is usually the most powerful reinforcer. The modifications should be aimed at permitting the students to complete each task well and successfully.

If students remain too much distracted and unengaged, seemingly indifferent to success, then the informal checklist of health, nutritional, emotional, and social problems must be used by teachers and counselors. The intervention then may best be planned by health or human services workers. We do reemphasize, the curriculum will be a primary cause in most cases and will be implicated in many others.

The first step in diagnostic testing after sensory screening should be the identification of individual entry-level skills and the observation of the student engaged there.

The Diagnostic Fallacy

Diagnostic testing can itself become an obstacle to improving the lot of learning disabled and low-achieving children. As has been emphasized previously, tests can affect the curriculum or instructional programs. When diagnostic tests are administered to students, it is assumed that the results will be honored by providing instruction in accordance with the deficiencies revealed on the tests. Diagnostic testing is done with the view of finding a deficiency—a shortcoming—that is interfering with learning.

When testing students who have been failing, inevitably deficiencies or weaknesses can be identified. Focusing on instructional activities to remediate these deficiencies can produce a great deal of frustration. Rather than focusing instructional activities on remediating deficiencies, the focus should be on identifying the student's entry or instructional level. Any instructional activities should be at the skill level comparable to the entry or instructional level, or slightly below if the student needs a high degree of success.

Remedial instruction should follow developmental curricular sequence and instructional level guidelines. Diagnostic testing should be focused on strengths, the threshold or baseline skill of students. These are frequently harder to identify, though, since most of our formal measurement systems are not designed to do this. Our current methods of diagnosis can lead to interventions which may prove to be difficult and frustrating for the student.

The other problem that diagnostic testing causes has to do with content validity. Diagnostic tests may have little content in common with the curriculum in use. Diagnostic testing can, consequently, form a new and different curriculum for a student, if the deficiency is noted in an area of such dissimilarity. There is an axiom used in curriculum-based assessment (Hargis, 1987) that applies to diagnostic testing: Choose your tests well, for they will become a curriculum.

A new curriculum based on diagnostic test results will displace instructional time in the regular curriculum. The regular curriculum is where the students' progress will be evaluated, but they may now be in the contradictory predicament of spending less time engaged in it because of diagnostic test results. Diagnostic testing can have the effect of diluting instructional effort and stalling achievement. Diagnostic testing should be curriculum-based. It usually should simply be a more detailed examination of curriculum constituents on the curriculum in use.

Self-Assessment

Testing is something that is usually done "to students." However, students should participate far more in their own assessment. Students should be as much engaged in monitoring their own progress as are their teachers. Students need to be as specifically aware as possible of what they are doing and where they are going. Self assessment helps the student be a more reflective, aware, and engaged learner. Students should be active in monitoring their own progress and setting reasonable attainable goals. There is every reason to believe that students can make reliable and valid judgments about their own skills and learning if this is a regular part of all learning activities.

The notion of self-assessment may seem to contradict standard assessment practices. It may seem that students do not have the skill to assess their own instructional needs and progress. However, in the most important aspects of instructional activity, elementary age children are quite capable of handling many assessment activities. The reader is well referred to a study by Kwang Seon Kim (1991) in which he studied the ability of both regular students and students with learning disabilities to assess their own word knowledge. Elementary age students with and without learning disabilities are quite accurate in identifying which words they know or don't know on isolated word lists and in the context of reading selections. This is the most important skill required in identifying the appropriate instructional level reading material and for identifying current reading level.

Students can tell for themselves when reading material is too hard to engage in with comprehension. They can and should learn to inventory their skills and attainments. They should learn to check, compare to standards, approximate, edit and revise; all these kinds of things are important parts of assessment. They are also important parts of active and reflective learning.

The monitoring of ongoing performance in existing curricula to make sure that students can effectively engage is the most fundamental part of assessment. Much of it should be done cooperatively with the students. Computerized assessment and instructional systems such as the CBA–ID system (Kim, 1991) can help make the process more efficient and effective.

Self-assessment as an integral part of instruction should be common policy. Students should be engaged in monitoring their own progress, seeking helpful corrective feedback, and in deciding what to engage in next.

Chapter 6

THE BEST ASSESSOR FOR PLANNING INSTRUCTION—THE TEACHER

Some school systems employ personnel who are recognized for their expertise in testing and assessment. These may include personnel with titles such as testing officer, diagnostician, assessment specialist, psychometrist, psychologist, etc. Each of these specialists usually have their own specialty or expertise in testing and assessment. For example, the testing officer may be very well informed regarding group-administered tests mandated by the state.

The specialty of the psychometrist or psychologist is usually that administering individually IQ tests and interpreting the results to determine if the student meets the criteria for receiving special services as established by state mandates.

Some of these assessment specialists, perhaps in an attempt to protect their own domain, promoted the idea that assessment requires specialized skills and can be performed only by the specialists. The promotion of this idea, and other factors, appear to have caused some teachers to feel incompetent regarding assessment. These teachers have the impression assessment should be left to the specialist(s).

The idea of leaving assessment to the assessment specialists is valid regarding some types of assessment. It is valid for the state-mandated norm-referenced testing program and IQ testing as in the above examples. However, this idea is not valid or realistic regarding assessment for planning instruction.

It is not unusual for assessment specialists such as those listed above to find their schedules completely occupied with duties and assessments which must be conducted solely to comply with state mandates. Realistically, the amount of time their schedules permit for conducting the type of assessment needed for planning instruction is usually very limited.

The training and experience of some of these specialists emphasized statistical methods and the interpretation of normative data. Thus, some of these specialists have a tendency to want to quantify results in order to make statistical interpretation. Those having this tendency are prone to interpret results quantitatively in terms of broader goals or areas. They may be much more prone to make these types of interpretations instead of how the results can be translated into instructional objectives.

The training and experience in curriculum development and teaching of some "testing specialists" are very limited. Some have limited insights regarding how the results relate to learning, the curriculum or any difficulty(ies) the student may be experiencing. Thus, their expertise in conducting assessment for instructional planning purposes may be limited compared to that of a competent teacher with a strong background in curriculum development and teaching.

Thus, the authors propose that realistically the teacher must assume the primary role for conducting assessment related to instructional planning. The rationale for proposing this position will be discussed in this chapter.

Are Teacher Assessments Valid?

As indicated above, some assessment specialists are prone to question the idea of a teacher playing a major role in assessment. Some are quick to challenge the teacher ability to derive valid assessment results.

True, teacher-developed assessment materials and assessment procedures used by most teachers do not comply with the criteria established by the American Psychological Association or other test construction criteria. However, this does not mean that these teachers cannot derive valid and useful assessment information for planning instruction.

Realistically, the teacher is in the "number one" position for deriving valid assessing results for instructional planning purposes. The teacher who has a strong background in curriculum development and has developed the skill of integrating assessment and instruction is the "expert" in conducting this type of assessment.

Numerous research studies have concluded the observant teacher's opinions regarding the skills of students are just as valid, and frequently more valid, than results derived from formal assessments. Why should these research findings have been expected? In most cases the teacher is the person who has the opportunity to observe and evaluate the most samplings of the student's behavior and performance. He/she is more likely to be the one who can observe behaviors and the performance of skills:

    a. in different contexts or settings.
    b. on several different days rather than just on "test day."
    c. when prerequisite skills are needed to perform a higher level skill.
    d. in a more relaxed and natural setting rather than in a testing situation which can be very anxiety producing for many students.

Because of the unique position of the teacher to base an assessment on a broader and larger sampling of the student's performance, the validity of such assessment is usually very adequate. The validity of the teacher's informal assessment may be greater than results derived from a limited sampling in a more formal assessment on "test day."

Teacher Assessments

1. Provide Valid Insights Regarding How Student/Teacher Rapport Can Be Developed

After completing an assessment, the specialist frequently shares the results with the teacher. In some cases the sharing of such information is routine and very helpful.

However, after initiating the student's instructional plan, the teacher may conclude the results reported by the specialist were not valid. Does this mean the assessment specialist was incompetent? No, not necessarily. Regardless of the competency level of the specialist, information derived from a formal assessment may prove to be invalid for different reasons such as those discussed above—limited sampling of skills, student having a "bad day," poor testing environment, etc.

The "chemistry" or rapport which exists between the student and the specialist may be very different from that which exists between the student and the teacher. For example, if the "chemistry" between the student and specialist was positive and the "chemistry" between the student and teacher tends to be negative, the teacher may conclude the student is more difficult to work with than the specialist indicated. If the reverse is true, the teacher may conclude the specialist's report was much too negative and suspect the specialist was unfair and biased against the student.

This difference in "chemistry" or rapport may be determined by several subtle factors, such as the student's previous experiences with people of the same age, sex, color, dress, or accent of the specialist or teacher. Yes, most competent specialists are aware that such subtle factors can affect rapport during an assessment. However, identifying such factors and determining to what degree they may lower the student's performance is not always possible even by the more competent specialist or teacher.

When the teacher performs the assessment, valuable insights can be obtained regarding the type of rapport which may exist between the teacher and the student. If the teacher conducts the assessment, insights may also be obtained as to how good rapport can be established with the student. This is not to imply the competent specialist could not gain insights regarding what techniques might be recommended for establishing rapport. Some specialists are very skilled at making such recommendations. The idea is that the teacher's firsthand experience with the student during the assessment is very likely to provide a better understanding of what rapport or "chemistry" is likely to exist between them. Then, during the assessment, the teacher can gain valuable insights regarding which techniques from his or her own "bag of tricks" will be the most effective in establishing good student/teacher rapport.

2. Avoid Misunderstandings or Misinterpretations That May Take Place in the Reporting Process

Another reason the teacher may conclude results reported by the specialist are invalid may be related to a lack of good communication between the specialist and the teacher. Valuable insights gained by the specialist during the assessment may be lost or distorted in the communication process—written or verbal.

The loss or distortion may take place for several reasons. First, there may be a lapse of time between the time the specialist completes the assessment and is able to verbally share the results with the teacher or write the report. As a result, some of the information may not be recalled. If the report is written, some of the information may be deleted for the sake of brevity. A very frequent complaint from teachers regarding written reports from specialists is the delay in receiving them. The teacher may be expected to begin working with the student prior to receiving the assessment report from the specialist. A loss or distortion in communication may be the result of differences in vocabulary or terminology used by the specialist and that used the teacher.

3. Permit the Integration of Assessment and Teaching

Assessment is a prerequisite of good teaching. Effective instruction and assessment are inseparable. Good teachers assess constantly by observing the responses and performances of their students. These daily observations provide the teacher with the unique opportunity of observing the student performing a skill on a daily basis and at the appropriate time. Such observations are often a much more valid assessment of skill mastery than a "one-time" performance of the skill(s) in a more structured, superficial or stressful assessment situation conducted by the "testing specialist."

The authors would propose that teachers who are capable of teaching a skill are equally capable of determining when the student has mastered the skill. Or, vice versa, if the teacher is not capable of determining if a student can perform a skill to be taught, the teacher is probably not capable of teaching the skill.

4. Result in the Most Appropriate and Helpful Assessments Being Conducted

The teacher is usually the person in the best position to know what skill areas need to be assessed. He/she may be the person who knows best what type of assessment will be more likely to yield the data needed for instructional planning.

Factors which determine how much time should be devoted to conducting assessment per se should be determined by the teacher. This amount of time should be determined by opportunities the teacher has had to observe the student performing skills in the daily program. This might include verbal responses during class discussion or an evaluation of daily written assignments.

To make the most efficient use of assessment time, an assessment should be initiated slightly below the skill level of the student. Not doing so may result in a waste of time. Initiating or conducting the assessment of skills far below the student's performance or skill level can also be an ineffective use of time.

An assessment should also be initiated at a skill level where the student can have a fair degree of success and not feel too threatened, traumatized or like a failure. The teacher is usually the person who is the most aware of the skill level appropriate for initiating the assessment.

5. Result In The Use Of The Most Efficient Administration Option(s)

In some situations there may be several options as to how an assessment is administered—individual administration with oral or written responses, group administration with written responses, teacher's observations or informal appraisal of the student's performance in the school or work setting, etc. The teacher may be the best qualified to determine which administration option is the best, as well as the best time and setting for administering the assessment.

With some text or programs including assessment materials, the teacher may have the material needed to conduct the assessment at his/her fingertips. In many cases, the teacher will be the one who knows this curriculum and assessment material best and how to use it in the most effective manner.

As much as possible, the skills should be assessed in a functional setting or lifelike situation—the setting, situations or environment which demands use of the skill. More frequently, this will be in a working relationship with the teacher. Again, the teacher is usually in the best position or role for accommodating the need for conducting the assessment in a functional setting or lifelike situation.

6. Result in Adaptations Needed or Crucial for Obtaining the Most Valid Assessment

When assessing some students, a valid assessment is possible only if adaptations are made. For example, the results of some assessments should not be considered valid if the student's reading skills are inadequate for reading and comprehending the directions and/or test items.

The teacher is likely to be the person who knows if directions need to be rephrased in order for the student to comprehend what skill is to be performed or demonstrated. For example, if the teacher (or material used in the school program) is always phrased "Write the answers for these addition problems" and the test directions are "Write the sums," the student may be confused and uncertain as to what skill is to be performed. The teacher should be aware of the need to rephrase the directions.

Rephrasing directions is one method or technique of obtaining a more valid assessment of the student's skills (when conducting an informal assessment). However, there may be times when rephrasing the direction still leaves doubt in the student's mind as to what skills are to be demonstrated—what response is expected. In such cases, providing an example or demonstrating the type of response expected may be the only means of communicating to the student what skill is to be demonstrated. The teacher may be the person most aware or sensitive to this need.

Other types of adaptations may be crucial to accommodate other handicaps—auditory, visual, short attention span, etc. Obviously, adaptations such as those mentioned above apply to informal assessment. These adaptations may not be appropriate or should be used more cautiously when conducting a norm-referenced assessment. Who is more likely to know about the need for these adaptations? Obviously an observant teacher is.

7. Provide More Insight Regarding The Validity of The Assessment

For several reasons unrelated to the student not possessing the skill being assessed, a student may perform poorly on an assessment. Who is more likely to know why the student may have failed to perform a skill of which the student possesses mastery for reasons such as a lack of confidence, difficulty in understanding directions, speech or language problem or reading difficulties (providing it is not a reading assessment)? It is the same person: the observant teacher.

The observant and alert teacher may be able to identify or hypothesize reasons for errors or failure resulting from variables unrelated to the skill being assessed. These might include factors such as:

- a "bad day" following a poor night's sleep,
- extreme test anxiety,
- a mere lack of interest or motivation, or
- defiance or resentment to the assessment.

Sometimes a student's response during an assessment clearly demonstrates mastery. However, this provides no assurance the student will apply or perform the demonstrated skills in a functional manner in his or her environment. The teacher will be the one most likely to be aware of this situation.

The validity of some assessment data may be questionable. When such is the case, the teacher may be able to make observations to confirm or disprove the validity of the data.

Shortcomings of Teacher Assessments

No doubt about it, the observant teacher who works closely with students is usually the best person in the best position to conduct assessment procedures for planning instruction. An effective teacher not only assesses weekly and daily but also at each stage or level as a lesson is presented.

He/she observes to see if the students' responses indicate they were comprehended. Questions to elicit responses are asked to determine if the information presented was understood by the student. The effective teacher continues to ask questions as a means of determining the need for review. Reasons from incorrect and inappropriate responses from students are evaluated.

However, teacher assessment is not without its shortcomings. Consequently, the teacher should be aware of poor practices or problems associated with teacher assessment.

Guidelines For Planning and Conducting Teacher Assessments

1. Guard Against Using Teaching Prompts Without Being Aware Of How Doing So Affects The Results

Although the authors' position is that continuous assessment is a prerequisite of effective teaching, the teacher must be aware that the purposes of each (assessing and teaching) are different. The manner in which each process is conducted may also be very different. For example, "modeling" and "guided practice" are frequently recognized as effective techniques of teaching. If an assessment is to be conducted to determine if a skill has mastered at the independent level, neither of these techniques should be performed. If the objective of instruction is that the skill will be performed independently, such prompts should not be provided during the assessment. Credit for mastery of a skill at the independent level should be granted only if the student demonstrates master without prompts—without a model, guidance, coaching, clues, etc.

Teachers who are prone to using frequent prompts, such as modeling, guidance, and coaching, when teaching are sometimes prone, consciously or unconsciously, to provide these same prompts when assessing. The authors have observed teachers providing such prompts without being aware of the prompts they are providing them. Providing such prompts is a habit or seemingly has become second nature with many effective teachers and they may unconsciously be using them when conducting an assessment. Thus, the teacher must continuously guard against using teaching prompts when assessing, as doing so may lead to invalid results.

Are prompts such as modeling, guided practice and coaching ever in order when conducting an assessment? Yes, definitely.

An assessment may reveal that the student *cannot* perform a skill at the independent level. When this is true, the teacher may need to know, "At what level or with what prompts and conditions can the skill be performed?" Is the student unable to perform the skills even when prompts are provided? Can the skill be performed when modeled or when guidance and coaching are given?

Deriving answers to such questions may be the purpose of some assessments. The answers derived may be crucial in determining the most effective method or level of instruction. For example, reteaching or modeling a skill will be an ineffective use of instructional time if guided practice or coaching is all the student needs to achieve mastery. Yes, practice (or drill) is an important prerequisite for the mastery of many skills. Some skills such as reading skills only become functional, integrated, automatic and retained on a long-term basis if practice is part of the teaching and learning process.

2. *Grant Credit for Mastery Only If Mastery is Unquestionable*

Some teachers tend to be too lenient in granting credit and may grant credit for mastery when adequate mastery is questionable. They may be prone to give credit for a skill mastered only at the "marginal" or "merging" level.

Credit for mastery should not be granted for skills mastered only at the merging, marginal or questionable level. The mastery of skills at these levels are usually not performed by the student in a functional or effective manner. When skills are mastered only at the merging or marginal level, retention is usually poor. Also, the student is more likely to have learning difficulties when these skills are needed as prerequisite skills which must be integrated with other skills in order to master high-level skills. Skills mastered only of these limited levels should be identified as instruction objectives. For these skills, an appropriate instructional objective might be to "Improve mastery from the marginal or emerging level to the functional and automatic level."

Perhaps one reason teachers are prone to give credit when mastery is questionable is because it is a common practice when administering norm-referenced assessment. When administering a norm-referenced or standardized test, most assessors tend to give the student the "benefit of any doubt(s)." This is a commonly accepted or recommended practice when administering a norm-referenced or standardized test.

The opposite practice is more appropriate when conducting criterion- or curriculum-based assessment. The recommended practice when conducting an assessment for planning instruction should be, "If in doubt, don't give credit. Continue to identify the skill as an instructional objective until there is not doubt of mastery."

3. Grant Credit Only If Mastery Is At the Automatic Or Functional Level

Another shortcoming frequently identified with teachers conducting assessment is giving credit for performing a skill which is not mastered at the automatic or functional level. For some skills, mastery at the automatic or functional level is crucial. If some skills are not mastered at the automatic level, they are not retained well. If some skills are not mastered at the functional level, they are of no value to the student and may cause the student to experience problems when attempting to use them in a functional manner in the environment.

For example, the student may be given credit for the mastery of number facts without mastery being at the automatic level. Such credit may have been given after the student responded with a high degree of accuracy when presented with a list of number facts and given an unlimited amount of time. Fingers may even be used in computing the answers. Mastery of the number facts only at this skill level will probably not be retained well, and the student is likely to experience difficulty when presented with higher-level math skills in the classroom.

To be successful in the classroom, the student should have mastery at the automatic level. This means the number facts can be recalled without a significant delay and taxing of the thought processes. The mastery of some skills will need to involve or include more than merely recalling (stating) information at the automatic level. To be functional, the student may need knowledge or insight as to how and when to apply the skill or information. As indicated above, credit for skill mastery should not be granted if there is any doubt of mastery. It is recommended that the skill continue to be identified as an instructional objective until performance rules out all doubts of mastery.

Some teachers are prone to give credit when the student merely "parrots" the correct response. If the student's response suggests mere "parroting" and a lack of comprehension, credit for skill mastery should not be granted. Teaching strategies should be directed toward helping students master the skill in a functional manner and good comprehension of the same.

4. Have a Good Understanding of the Curriculum

In order to conduct informal curriculum-based assessment in the most effective manner, the teacher should have a good understanding of the curriculum. Having a good understanding of the curriculum involves more than merely knowing the goals and objectives stated in the curriculum guide. It also involves the ability to task-analyze the different skill levels, subskills and prerequisite skills the student must master in order to reach (achieve) the stated goals and objectives. Thus, the teacher with limited skills for performing a task analysis on what is to be taught (mastered) cannot be expected to do a superb job in conducting curriculum-based assessment.

5. Focus On Identifying the Skills Level
For Initiating Instruction—Avoid Letting
the Assessment Become Exhaustive

Some teachers tend to think they are not doing adequate assessment unless they identify everything there is to know about the skills of a student. They may feel compelled to continue assessing until an exhaustive listing of what the student knows and does not has be obtained. This tendency or practice can be counterproductive and result in ineffective use of time. The time involved in conducting an exhaustive assessment may be at the expense of time which could better be spent as instructional time.

In some cases the student may become impatient, annoyed and resentful of an extensive or exhaustive assessment. A preferred practice would be to limit the initial assessment to identifying the skill level at which instruction should be initiated. Then, after instruction had been initiated, assessment can become an ongoing process. One of the fallacies and problems encountered in many special education programs in recent years was the mandating of an IEP based on an exhaustive initial assessment. The model suggested or mandated in some of these programs was on an annual basis. The teacher was expected to conduct an assessment which would yield enough instructional objectives for an entire school year. Conducting such an exhaustive assessment and compiling a yearlong list of objectives for the IEP proved to be exhaustive to the teacher and involved too much paperwork. It was an ineffective use of time.

A preferred approach would have been to focus on identifying the skill level for initial instruction. Then, without delaying instruction to spend more time assessing, initiate instruction with plans for embedding or integrating ongoing assessing in the instructional program as needed. This ongoing assessment can be accommodated by analyzing the student's error patterns, behavior, interest(s), rate of performance, etc., in the daily instructional program.

Chapter 7

EFFECTIVE CURRICULUM-BASED ASSESSMENT

Effective assessment, like effective teaching, requires planning. First, a clearly defined purpose is essential. Otherwise, much time can be wasted and the results may be worthless or serve no purpose.

The purpose determines:

a. the type of assessment which will be done—informal or structured observation, norm-referenced testing, criterion-referenced assessment, curriculum-based assessment, etc.
b. what activities or procedures may need to be performed prior to planning and initiating the assessment.
c. specific skill areas which may need to be assessed.
d. skill levels which will probably need to be the focus.

General Guidelines for Effective Assessment

When conducting assessment for planning instruction, each situation has its own purpose(s), limitations and constraints. Thus, it would not be appropriate to recommend following a rigidly prescribed and standardized set of rules as is usually true with norm-referenced assessment. However, following certain guidelines such as the ones listed and discussed below is likely to result in a more effective use of time and yield more effective results.

1. Analyze Available Student Data

The time spent conducting an assessment is usually a waste of time if it only yields information or data someone else already knows. Thus, to use assessment time in the most effective manner, the assessor should collect and analyze what student data is available. This may include analyzing student work samples; interviewing a previous teacher, the parent, or the student; etc. Analyzing such data may provide a great deal of insight as to the most appropriate skill level for initiating a curriculum-based assessment. This is not to imply the validity of data received from others should be considered as unquestionable. In some cases, it may be appropriate to use some assessment time for confirming or refuting the validity of such data. Analyzing available student data may be essential in order to formulate a well-defined purpose for conducting an assessment.

2. Strive for a Well-Defined Purpose and Understanding of What the Outcome Should Be

The teacher often finds a student in his or her class to be a challenge, a concern or a frustration. The teacher may refer such a student for an assessment without having a clear understanding of the real purpose of the assessment and what the possible outcome(s) from the assessment might be.

When this happens it is usually crucial for the person receiving the referral or request for assessment to consult with the referring or requesting teacher. The purpose of this consultation should be to formulate a well-defined purpose for the referral or request. Consultation with the referring teacher should result in an understanding of possible actions or outcomes which may take place as a result of the assessment. What outcome(s) or course action(s) is the referring teacher expecting from the referral? Are the results of the assessment likely to result in action, such as the:

   a. referring teacher being provided with assessment data and expected to provide an individualized program based on the assessment data?
   b. student being placed in a remedial program?
   c. student remaining in the referring teacher's class and provided with special tutoring, assistance, or support?

Following a review of available student and consultation with the referring teacher, it is not unusual to conclude that some other course of action may be more appropriate than immediately initiating an assessment. If a well-defined purpose for the assessment cannot be formulated, alternate actions such as observations, trying a different instructional strategy or a parent conference may be a better use of time. It may be best to delay the assessment until other alternatives have been tried or the data needed to formulate a well-defined purpose is available.

3. Plan to Confirm the Proficiency Level Of Reported Skills, If Questionable

A review of student data may indicate what skills have been mastered. However, the student's mastery of some of these skills may not be at the automatic or functional level. Other skills may have been mastered at these levels at one time but may need to be reviewed or practiced. For example, available data may suggest Timothy has mastered decoding skills and word-recognition skills. However, the "reason for referral for assessment" states "Timothy is having difficulty with second grade reading."

A significant part of the assessment may include confirming at what rate or proficiency level Timothy has mastered decoding and word-recognition skills. The following two questions will serve as a guide in making this assessment. Can these skills be performed at a slower rate if Timothy uses "90% of his reasoning power" to perform them? Or, can Timothy perform these skills at a faster rate, seemingly by using only "10% of his reasoning power"?

If Timothy must use "90% of his reasoning power" to decode second grade material and his performance is at a slower rate, he can*not* be expected to be a proficient reader. This means he only has "10% of his reasoning power" left to use for other reading skills such as comprehending what is read. If Timothy's reading rate is significantly decreased because of delays in decoding too many unknown words, his ability to read with comprehension will be decreased significantly.

The Commission on Reading (1985) in their report, *Becoming A Nation of Readers,* list fluency as one of the five principles of reading. The report states, "Readers must be able to decode words quickly and accurately so that the process can coordinate fluidly with the process of constructing the meaning of the text." This report stresses that a decoding skill must be developed to the automatic level so very little conscious attention is required to perform the skills. Fluency and comprehension are possible only when decoding skills are developed to this degree. The simple explanation for this finding is that the reader's attention must be available to interpret the text rather than to figure out (decode) unfamiliar words.

Most authorities on teaching readers agree that to become a proficient reader the student must have the skills of recognizing words automatically with little conscious attention. However, there is not complete agreement as to what criteria should be used regarding the rate. The

Commission on Reading reports that available figures suggest the criteria for an average third grader should be that of "reading aloud an unfamiliar story at the rate of about 100 or more words per minute." The authors know some first grade teachers use the criteria of at least one word per second and concur that this rate be considered an acceptable criteria.

Likewise, a student may be proficient at using context clues to figure out (decode) unknown words. However, if the student's automatic recognition of high-frequency words is so limited he must pause to figure out one or two words in each sentence by using "phonic" clues, reading becomes very taxing. Reading is "not fun," is not rewarding and the student tires quickly.

The authors' position is that a student cannot be a proficient reader if "90% of the reasoning power" must be focused on figuring out unknown works by context or by decoding. This means only "10% of the reasoning power" is left for comprehending the text.

The above is not to be taken or interpreted literally. There is no precise method for determining if a student is using "90% of his or her reasoning power" to perform a skill such as decoding unknown words. Such estimation or conclusion must be based on the teacher's judgment after listening to the student orally read a passage written at a designated grade level. As the passage is read, the teacher may find it helpful to determine the student's reading rate (words per minute) and record error analysis. It is usually best if such an evaluation can be made without the student being aware of it.

Yes, a great deal of teacher assessment can and should be made without the student being aware of it or made to feel "This is a test." Rather than clicking a stopwatch or using other timing procedures which are obvious to the student, more subtle timing procedures should be used. Such procedures may involve the teacher glancing at a watch, hopefully without the student being aware of it, even if such timing procedures may not be as accurate as using a stopwatch.

The Commission on Reading reports that although fluency is an important principle in learning to read, it is frequently not assessed by standardized tests. The commission points out that this is a major shortcoming in using standardized tests as a means of improving the teaching of reading.

4. Use Norm-Referenced Assessment Only If There Is A Mandate To Do So

Norm-referenced tests are developed and used primarily for comparing a student's performance to the performance of a peer group on which the test was standardized. The results derived will probably indicate the underachiever is not achieving as well as his or her peer group, which is probably what the teacher already knew or at least suspected.

Administering a norm-referenced test may yield an amazing amount of numerical data—raw score, grade-equivalent, percentile, stanine, etc.—which usually takes a great deal of time to compute and record. However, the main reason that administering the norm-referenced test is not an effective use of time is because this numerical data cannot be translated into instructional plans—the skill level(s) at which instruction should be initiated. Thus, when conducting an assessment solely for the purpose of planning instruction for underachievers, norm-referenced tests are typically inappropriate and a waste of valuable time.

However, normative student data is required to meet the mandates of some programs—eligibility, funding, documenting progress quantitatively, etc. Such requirements usually lead to the mandating of norm-referenced test(s). Such mandates leave no alternative. If norm-referenced tests are mandated, the authors' first recommendation would be to select and use the norm-referenced test which will take the least time to administer and score. If norm-referenced testing is mandated, don't chalk it up as a total waste of time. Study the student's responses to the test items to analyze error patterns, reasons for incorrect responses, and the skill level of items on which the student begins to have difficulty. This type of information may provide an approximation of the student's skill level(s). Thus, it may be helpful in determining the skill level(s) for initiating criterion-referenced assessment as discussed below.

5. Use Criterion-Referenced Assessment For More Useful Information

Criterion-referenced assessment is designed for measuring what skill(s) the student has mastered, and *not* for yielding quantitative data as with norm-referenced test as discussed above. Thus, criterion-referenced assessment yields information which can be translated into what to teach—the skill level(s) at which instruction should be initiated.

Criterion-referenced tests are available commercially or they may be teacher designed. Both have their advantages and disadvantages. Most commercially designed instruments have explicit directions for administration and scoring. However, it is the authors' opinion that teachers have tended to be more rigid in following these exact procedures than they should be. No doubt the tendency to want to administer tests rigidly is a carry-over from using norm-referenced tests. When administering a norm-referenced test, explicit directions and scoring must be followed or the numerical results cannot be considered as valid.

The authors prefer not to think of the material used for criterion-referenced assessment as "tests" but as instruments or inventories. One of the authors is the developer of the BRIGANCE® Inventories. These Inventories include student materials and procedures for criterion-referenced assessment of several skill areas and levels. The authors' experience has been that personnel who have a tendency to refer to or think of the BRIGANCE® Inventories as "tests" tend to:

    a. have more difficulty understanding the purposes of the instruments (example: wanting to derive quantitative data more than information regarding the student's mastery level),

    b. overuse them (the Inventories)—not able to overcome the "whole test syndrome" and not being selective as to what assessments would be more likely to yield the most helpful information in the least amount of time,

    c. feel compelled to administer them rigidly (as if using a norm-referenced test), and

    d. be very reluctant to use teacher judgment regarding making adaptations and interpretations.

Personnel who viewed the Inventories as their curriculum-based assessment instruments rather than as tests typically did not experience the difficulties listed above. They use them much more effectively by:

    a. adapting the assessments to accommodate different situations—observations, group administration, integrating them into the instructional program.

    b. using them much more informally, selectively and with adaptations which would yield the most helpful information regarding the student's mastery level.

The authors believe that when conducting a criterion-referenced assessment it is crucial the teacher take a very different approach than when administering a norm-referenced test. When doing criterion-referenced assessment the teacher's primary concern should *not* be following explicit directions as stated in the manual. Instead of using rigid administration procedures, the authors recommend the teacher feel more freedom to deviate from the directions if there is reason to believe doing so is likely to yield more helpful information.

For example, the "Directions to the student" (as printed in the manual of commercially prepared criterion-referenced materials) may be "Write the sums for these problems." The student's response makes it obvious there is confusion regarding the meaning of "sum." In such situations the teacher should feel complete freedom to rephrase the directions to "Write the answers to these addition problems." Doing so may be the only way of "putting the student at ease" and identifying what addition computational skills the student can perform. The teacher may wish to make a note that part of the student's instructional plan should include developing the concept of "sum."

Teacher-made criterion-referenced materials can be very effective and are recommended. Such materials can be tailored to concur with the instructional program and can be tailored to be more effective in meeting the needs of the teacher. Teacher-made criterion-referenced material can have some drawbacks. Developing and revising/perfecting such materials can be extremely time consuming. This is time which might best be spent planning for more effective instruction.

Some teachers lack experience with a task-analytic approach, and, if so, this inexperience is likely to be reflected in a poor quality of material developed. Another shortcoming of teacher-made criterion-referenced material is likely to be poor graphics. Most teachers do not have the resources (equipment, materials, supplies and skills) needed to develop and reproduce quality visual/graphic material. For example, if teacher-made material is produced on equipment with print or font of smaller size than is appropriate for primary children and then reproduced with poor imagery, some students will find it difficult to read.

Some instructional programs include criterion-referenced assessment material. The teacher may find it convenient or more expedient to excerpt some of this material from the program and place it in a binder.

The above discussion does not to imply that criterion-referenced material cannot be simple. For assessing some skills it can be very simple. Resourceful teachers frequently sequence simple material such as flashcards in a skill hierarchy and use them for conducting a criterion-referenced assessment.

The authors have, in a very informal manner, conducted criterion-referenced assessment by writing computational problems of a skill hierarchy on the chalkboard and asking the student to compute the answers. Such simple techniques certainly can have their advantages. These simple techniques not only allow assessment to be done on a limited budget, but they can prove to be very natural stress-free assessment situation for the student.

6. Arrange for An Effective Recording and Recordkeeping System

A problem frequently associated with teacher assessment is that of having a method or means of recording assessment results — the need for a recordkeeping system. Recording, as well as reading and interpreting, assessment data can be very time consuming. The authors have observed and known some teachers who can retain an enormous amount of data about the skills of their student in their minds. Being able to do so is a valuable asset:

  a. if the teacher can recall the data when needed.
  b. as recordkeeping can be time consuming.

However, in many situations there will be the need to record this data. This recorded data may be needed as a method of communicating to other teachers, the parents or when making a referral.

The use of a "uniform" student profile sheet which includes the major curriculum areas and skills is usually much less time consuming. This may be a locally developed profile. Commercially prepared materials such as the Student Record Books in the BRIGANCE® Inventories are also available for this purpose. These Student Record Books include major areas of the curriculum and the major skills within each curriculum area. They have been designed so the recordkeeping can be color-coded to provide an ongoing recordkeeping system which is easy to interpret.

The Student Record Books are correlated with the BRIGANCE® Inventories but can be used informally for recordkeeping purposes, if needed. The Brigance System also has a Class Record Book to serve as a recordkeeping system for an entire class. The Class Record Book may be used independently of the rest of the system and adapted to meet the teacher's needs.

7. Organize and Prepare

Just as with instruction, organizing and preparing for an assessment is essential. The importance of being organized and prepared cannot be overstated for successful teaching, and the same applies for effective assessment.

Prior to arrival of the student(s), all assessment materials for both the student(s) and the teacher should be at hand. If materials to be used for the later part of the assessment might be distracting when conducting the first part of the session, this material should be placed out of sight. The materials should be organized so it is convenient and available for presenting without delay at the appropriate time.

The teacher should review and know the procedures that will be followed in presenting the assessment items so they can be presented in a "natural" fashion. The teacher should also be familiar with where and how data is to be recorded to make certain the assessment session goes smoothly. Having the material organized well and being familiar with it means there will be less demand on the teacher's attention while conducting the assessment. This will make it possible for the teacher to focus more attention on:

a. establishing and maintaining a positive rapport with the student,
b. observing the student and evaluating the student's responses, and
c. recording the student's responses and observations made by the assessor.

Then there is the management of the physical environment as well as scheduling of time for the teacher and the student(s). Arranging for a good physical environment in some schools can be a major challenge. Foremost in arranging the assessment situation should be the student's physical comfort. This would include arranging for furniture that is of the correct size(s) and height(s) and a well-lit working area which is neither too hot nor too cold. Arranging to have a comfortable temperature and proper lighting may require advanced arrangements and planning.

As much as possible, schedule the assessment when it is anticipated the student will perform best. Other activities in which the student may be involved can make this difficult. The best performance cannot be

COMPREHENSIVE RECORD BOOK

Student's Name: _____ Birth Date: _____ Telephone: _____
Parents: _____ School/Program: _____
Home Address: _____ Address: _____
Comments: _____

RECORDING PROCEDURES AND COLOR CODE

Mark each evaluation in a different color to develop a graphic profile of progress.
- **Circle** skills for which mastery is demonstrated.
- **Underline** objectives to be mastered by the next evaluation with the next color as listed below.
- See page xi of the *Comprehensive Inventory of Basic Skills* for further discussion.

Testing Observations
Write the letters "S" or "N" and circle "Yes" or "No" in the designated box to describe the student's responses during testing. Use a pencil or pen of the color indicated on the left.

S - Satisfactory   N - Needs to improve

Evaluation	Color	Date	Examiner	Cooperation	Persistence	Attention Span	Concentration	Confidence	Rapport	Apparently Good Hearing	Apparently Good Vision
1st	Pencil									Yes No	Yes No
2nd	Blue									Yes No	Yes No
3rd	Red									Yes No	Yes No
4th	Black									Yes No	Yes No
5th	Green									Yes No	Yes No
6th	Purple									Yes No	Yes No

Comments: _____

© 1983 Curriculum Associates, Inc. 5 Esquire Rd. North Billerica MA 01862-2589. The **COMPREHENSIVE INVENTORY OF BASIC SKILLS** by Albert H. Brigance, the correlated **COMPREHENSIVE RECORD BOOK** and **COMPREHENSIVE CLASS RECORD BOOK**, and inventory process are patent pending. No part of this book may be reproduced in any form or by any means without permission in writing from the publisher. All rights reserved. BRIGANCE® is a trademark of Curriculum Associates Inc. ISBN 0-89187-681-2 Printed in the United States of America

A. Readiness (continued)

ASSESSMENT	PAGE		
A-23	35	**JOINS SETS:** Joins groups of like objects:	[k]3 [1]4 5 6 7 8 9 10[2]
A-24	36	**UNDERSTANDS NUMBERS:** Shows quantities to match number symbols:	[k]1 2 3 4 5 [1]6 7 8 9 10[2]
A-25	37	**NUMBERS IN SEQUENCE:** Writes numbers in sequence from memory to:	[k]3 5 [1]10 20 30 40 50 60 70 80 90 100[2]
A-26	38	**PRINTS PERSONAL DATA:**	[k]1. first name 2. middle name 3. last name [1]4. age 5. telephone number 6. address[2]
A-27	39	**PRINTS LOWERCASE LETTERS IN SEQUENCE:**	[k]a b c d e f g h i j k l m n o p q r s t u v w x y z[1]
A-28	39	**PRINTS UPPERCASE LETTERS IN SEQUENCE:**	[k]A B C D E F G H I J K L M N O P Q R S T U V W X Y Z[1]
A-29	40	**PRINTS LOWERCASE LETTERS DICTATED:**	[1]o a d g q b p c e l t i f j n m r h u v w y x z k s[2]
A-30	40	**PRINTS UPPERCASE LETTERS DICTATED:**	[1]O A D G Q B P C E L T I F J N M R H U V W Y X Z K S[2]
A-31	41-42	**RESPONSE TO AND EXPERIENCE WITH BOOKS:**	

[k]1. Describes actions shown in pictures.
2. Takes part in reading by inserting words and phrases.
3. Gains information from books about real things.
4. Attempts to "read" familiar books from memory.
5. Indicates an interest in books of humor, fantasy, growth, and "why" books.
6. Likes to follow along in book as it is read.

7. Attempts to read by looking at pictures.
8. Reads some words by sight.
9. Attempts to read words by using word-attack skills.
[1]10. Reads simple stories aloud.
11. Distinguishes between fantasy and reality in stories.
12. Reads at least one primer or read-to-me type of book, recognizing at least 95% of the words.[2]

Notes: _____

expected from the student who is concerned about missing lunch, a classroom party or a favorite crafts activity.

Then there are scheduling conflicts with other activities taking place in the school. This may involve scheduling at a time when there are no distractions such as band practice in an adjoining room or an active, noisy playground outside the window.

8. Strive For the Student's Best Performance

The teacher should take precautions to arrange for an assessment which fosters the student's best performance. This definitely includes arranging for a comfortable physical environment which is free from distractions as discussed above. It also involves striving for a situation which will be as anxiety-free as possible. Plan for and allow time to putting the student at ease regarding the assessment. Attempt to establish and maintain good communication and rapport. It is best to refrain from using the word "test," and usually there is no need to do so. The word tends to be stress- or anxiety-producing for most underachievers.

As much as the situation allows, present the assessment in a routine lesson fashion. Typically, it is sufficient to provide an explanation such as:

> "I need you to do some things for me. Some of the things I will ask you to do will be easy. Some things I ask you to do will be harder. Do as well as you can. I want you to do your best."

After introducing the assessment situation in a fashion as stated above, pause to see if the student appears to have some questions. Permit any questions and discuss them in an attempt to allay any fears or anxieties the student may have.

As the assessment progresses, provide praise as needed. If the student appears to need a high degree of success, spend more time on the easier skill levels as a means of providing the feeling of success. If the student seems confident and appears to need a challenge, tend to "test up" quicker than you would with the student who lacks confidence and appears to need a high degree of success.

9. Initiate the Assessment By Using a "Survey Assessment"

To make the most efficient use of assessment time, the assessment should usually be initiated by using a survey assessment. The purpose of such a survey is to obtain a broad sampling of the student's skills. This survey should provide the teacher with an overview of the skills the student seems to have mastered and those which seem to be lacking. The results from this survey should provide insight as to what skill level the in-depth assessment should be initiated.

An example of such a survey is the "Whole Numbers Computation Survey—Form A." This survey samples a broad range of basic computational skills. The publisher of the BRIGANCE® Comprehensive Inventory of Basic Skills grants permission to reproduce the survey in quantities as needed for non-profit educational purposes. Thus, copies may be reproduced for administering the survey individually or by group with a written response.

It is recommended the teacher use discretion as to how much of the survey is presented to the student(s). This should be determined by what the teacher knows about the student's grade level, math skills, frustration level, attention span, etc. For example, if the survey is being used with a group of second graders who have not been taught multiplication and division, the reproduced pages may be cut in half so that only the addition and subtraction problems are presented.

When assessing on an individual basis, the teacher may wish to ask the student to respond orally. This may be done informally by pointing to a problem and making requests, such as "Tell me how you would work this problem?"

The results from this survey will help the teacher identify the student's approximate skill level. By analyzing the response from this survey the teacher can identify possible causes for errors—poor handwriting, does not place numerals in the correct position, has not mastered addition number facts, has not mastered subtraction number facts, no concept of regrouping (carrying and borrowing), errors in regrouping (once, twice, without zero, with one zero, with two zeros, etc.), etc.

Even though the response to the survey is typically written, observations can still provide valuable insights. Observations of how a student responds when the survey is presented may reveal the student's level of confidence regarding math and willingness to accept a challenge. Observations made during the survey may reveal deficits such as a short attention span, or the need to use fingers or tally marks to compute answers.

DIRECTIONS: Write the answer for each subtraction fact. Work as quickly as you can without making mistakes. **NAME:**_____

1.
6 - 1 = ____
4 - 3 = ____
3 - 2 = ____
0 - 0 = ____
5 - 4 = ____
6 - 5 = ____
6 - 6 = ____
5 - 3 = ____
4 - 0 = ____
5 - 2 = ____

2.
7 - 5 = ____
8 - 4 = ____
7 - 3 = ____
7 - 6 = ____
8 - 2 = ____
7 - 7 = ____
7 - 4 = ____
8 - 3 = ____
8 - 0 = ____
8 - 6 = ____

3.
10 - 9 = ____
10 - 6 = ____
9 - 4 = ____
9 - 1 = ____
9 - 6 = ____
10 - 5 = ____
9 - 3 = ____
10 - 7 = ____
10 - 2 = ____
10 - 4 = ____

4.
12 - 6 = ____
11 - 5 = ____
11 - 3 = ____
12 - 3 = ____
12 - 7 = ____
12 - 10 = ____
11 - 9 = ____
11 - 7 = ____
12 - 4 = ____
12 - 8 = ____

5.
13 - 2 = ____
14 - 4 = ____
14 - 9 = ____
13 - 11 = ____
14 - 8 = ____
13 - 4 = ____
13 - 8 = ____
14 - 5 = ____
13 - 5 = ____
14 - 11 = ____

6.
15 - 3 = ____
16 - 7 = ____
16 - 5 = ____
15 - 9 = ____
15 - 8 = ____
16 - 3 = ____
16 - 9 = ____
16 - 11 = ____
15 - 5 = ____
15 - 12 = ____

7.
17 - 9 = ____
18 - 15 = ____
18 - 5 = ____
17 - 15 = ____
17 - 5 = ____
19 - 7 = ____
17 - 8 = ____
19 - 10 = ____
18 - 9 = ____
17 - 12 = ____

10. Initiate Low and "Test Up"

When initiating an assessment with items which have been sequenced by a skill hierarchy or difficulty level, attempt to initiate the assessment at the highest level you anticipate the student will perform error-free. This practice is appropriate when administering a survey assessment or the in-depth assessment discussed below.

Initiating the assessment at this skill or difficulty level will save time. It will aid in providing the student with the feel of success and confidence which is crucial for many students. Initiating the assessment at a higher level will likely make the student ill at ease and lessen the motivation or willingness to perform.

Based on the student's response to the first item—success or failure, deciding whether to "test down" or "test up" is usually apparent. If the student's response is unsuccessful, the need to "test down" is indicated in order to avoid the assessment becoming a stressful and anxiety-producing situation. The question then becomes, "How far down?" For many students who have been unsuccessful on the first item, success on the second item may be crucial. Following failure on the first item, having success on several consecutive items may be crucial in helping the student regain confidence. Thus, it is best to overestimate "How far down?" than to underestimate and have failure repeated on the second item.

If the "test down" is overestimated, adjustment can usually be made quickly. The student usually responds quickly to the items. Also, items may be skipped as you begin "testing up," perhaps administering every other item. This is especially true if you think the student is ready for more challenging items.

If the student appears to need lots of success, this can be provided by administering more of the easy items instead of moving quickly to the more difficult items and providing more praise for correct responses. Proceed "testing up" until the student begins to fail items.

Some authorities recommend "testing up" until the student performance is "error-full"—there is failure on several consecutive items. This is especially true of authorities with a strong background in norm-referenced testing where the practice is to test to the limits, the frustration level or and "error-full" ceiling has been established. The authors recommend this practice *not* be used with criterion-referenced or curriculum-based assessment involving a hierarchy of skills. Doing so will probably:

a. be counterproductive regarding student rapport,
b. take time,
c. may result in suggesting instruction should be initiating at the student's frustration level.

The preferred practice when assessing for planning instruction is to "test up" only to the skill level where the performance is no longer "error-free" and the student is beginning to experience failure and frustration. Do *not* continue the assessment to the frustration or complete failure level as if administering a norm-referenced test. Following the practice of discontinuing the assessment when performance ceases to be "error-free" and prior to failure producing student frustration and anxiety may yield results suggesting instruction should be initiated at a level below the student's comfortable level. However, initiating at this level is very much preferred over initiating instruction above the student's comfortable instructional level.

Initiating instruction slightly below the student's comfortable level can have several advantages, such as:

a. providing a review of some skills which may be very helpful or crucial prior to receiving instruction at a higher-level skill.

b. allowing the student to work more independently and develop more self-confidence.
c. the work not being so mentally taxing, and thus allowing the student to develop better study habits and a better attention span.
d. letting the teacher decide when and at what rate "teaching up" should take place in order to better meet the needs of the student.

11. Follow Up With a More Precise In-Depth Assessment Using Probes

From the results of the survey the teacher gains insight as to the most appropriate level for conducting the in-depth or probing assessment. This in-depth or probing assessment should focus on:

a. confirming possibly errors identified by the survey,
b. identifying skills which have not been mastered at functional or automatic level, and
c. identifying the level for initiating instruction.

For example, if the student's response to the survey suggests the possibility of a lack of mastery of some of the subtraction facts at the functional or automatic level, part of the in-depth assessment should include an assessment of subtraction facts.

The assessment can be administered individually or by group with a written response by presenting a reproduced copy of the assessment. In some situations the individual assessment might be administered more expediently by asking the student to respond verbally by stating the facts for each combination. These facts have been grouped by the quantity of the minuend. In order to save time when administering the assessment on an individual basis, you may wish to initiate the assessment one level below what you anticipate the student's level of difficulty to be. For example, if an analysis of errors on the survey suggested that Timothy began making errors for facts with minuends of 14, you may be able to save time by initiating the assessment for facts with minuends of 11 and 12.

After initiating the assessment, "test down" or "test up" as appropriate, depending on the student's response—significantly delayed or incorrect, or quick and correct. If the student's response is incorrect, significantly delayed or not given confidently, "test down" by refocusing the assessment to a lower skill level. If the student's response is accurate, quick and

DIRECTIONS: Do as many of the problems as you can. Be sure to work carefully and do as the signs tell you.

NAME: _____

1. a. 37   b. 72   c. 452   d. 387   e. 287   f. 3946
   +41   +19   +143   +442   +549   +2087

2. a. 76   b. 62   c. 686   d. 382   e. 573   f. 4003
   −23   −27   −243   −234   −495   −2326

3. a. 34   b. 58   c. 347   d. 733   e. 428   f. 421
   × 2   × 4   × 35   × 40   ×387   ×308

4. a. 4)29̄   b. 26)84̄   c. 24)144̄   d. 28)812̄   e. 292)7592̄   f. 214)8560̄

given with confidence, test up by refocusing the assessment to a higher skill level.

Whether "testing down" or "testing up," the best practice is to refocus the assessment one skill level below what you anticipate the student's mastery level to be. If after refocusing the assessment level the student responds successfully, "test up" to pinpoint the student's mastery level. For example, if it becomes obvious Timothy has not mastered the facts with minuends of 11 and 12, immediately refocus the assessment to a lower skill level—perhaps for facts with minuends of 9 and 10. If the opposite is true—Timothy responds quickly, accurately and confidently to a few of the facts with minuends of 11 and 12—say, "Tim you are doing great." Then "test up" by refocusing the assessment on a higher skill level—a level you think will help identify Timothy's mastery level in the least amount of time.

It is the authors' recommendation that mastery not be granted for a skill level unless the student can respond to the "Subtraction Facts" at a rate of at least one each correct response each three seconds. If the entire assessment is administered by group administration, it is recommended the student be granted credit for the highest skill level completed accurately in three minutes. Again, observations may provide almost as much insight as the written responses. Observations may reveal how the student responds to being timed or if the student needs to use "aids" such as fingers or tally marks to compute the answer.

The results from the assessment, based on correct responses as well as observations, should identify the level at which instruction should be initiated. For example, if the assessment reveals the student has mastery at the automatic level for the skills assessed in "boxes 1–5" (minuends to 14) but not for the items in "box 6" (minuends of 15 and 16), part of the initial instructional plan should include practicing subtraction facts with minuends of 15 and 16 until mastery is at the automatic level.

In broad terms, the automatic level is defined as being able to respond to the items without undue delay or without using a great deal of reasoning power. In more precise terms, the automatic level for "Subtraction Facts" might best be defined as the student being able to respond to the items at a rate of at least one item each three seconds, with an accuracy of at least 90% and without using "aids/crutches" such as tally marks.

Mastery at this proficiency level will "free up" more of the student's reasoning power when computing subtraction problems. It will prevent "overload" when computing subtraction problems. Thus, the student with mastery at this proficiency level will:

a. have more reasoning power to devote to the comprehension of the problems,
b. not tire so quickly,
c. feel more successful and confident, and
d. be more likely to complete math assignments within the allotted or expected time.

The opposites of the above are likely to occur with the student who has not mastered "Subtraction Facts" at the automatic level when presented with the simplest subtraction problems.

In summary, the effective plan for curriculum-based assessment includes:

1. Analyzing available student data.
2. Striving for a well-defined purpose and understanding of what the outcome may be.
3. Planning to confirm the proficiency level of reported skills, if questionable.

4. Using norm-referenced assessment only if there is a mandate to do so.
5. Using criterion-referenced assessment for more useful information.
6. Arranging for an effective recording and recordkeeping system.
7. Organizing and preparation in order for the assessment to go smoothly.
8. Striving for the student's best performance.
9. Initiating the assessment by using a "survey assessment."
10. Initiating the assessment low and "testing up."
11. Following up with a more precise in-depth assessment using probes.

Chapter 8

TESTS FOR ACCOUNTABILITY

There is no shortage of critics who point out the shortcomings of the public schools. These critics include numerous groups ranging from parents, employers and politicians. These critics are demanding higher standards of achievement. As these demands for higher standards are made, school authorities frequently demand funding for more resources.

Accountability frequently becomes the key word in the discussion of these demands. Accountability, as used in this discussion, means educators are to be accountable for using the financial resources received to improved school programs so students will achieve the standards the public is demanding. Obviously, this accountability will needed to be documented by some form of measurement. Whatever the specifics of these standards are, they will have to be translated into tests and into curricula that insure that the standards are attained.

We view the current turmoil over standards and assessment with some cynicism. The prevailing notion is that better tests and higher standards will make for higher achievement. We feel that this attitude is unlikely to improve achievement. There are several reasons for the opinion we hold.

We already give plenty of achievement tests. We give more tests than any other country by far. The tests are about as good as can be expected. After all, they are good enough to show that the performance of our students is inferior to the students in all other industrialized countries. Why should we try to develop different tests which will tell us essentially the same thing? We already have *The Iowa Test of Basic Skills, The California Achievement Test, The Metropolitan Achievement Tests,* and others. Now we have the *NAEP* which samples achievement every few years. These tests already tell us about how well our students do on specific content compared to each other and to students in other countries.

These tests sample the content of various curricula about as well as we are capable of doing at the moment. This is not to say that we can't do a better job of describing and identifying curricular content. However, without a uniform national standard curriculum, the content validity of tests can only be generally reflective of some basic academic areas. The likelihood of getting some national consensus on curricular content is, as we have discussed already, remote, except in some narrow basic skill areas dealing with computation and language arts.

We have enough norm-referenced tests currently to know how our students do as compared to others in various academic areas. Even if we had national standards and national standardized tests to explicitly measure achievement on those standards, we would only be able to more explicitly state the strengths and deficiencies. The tests and standards would do nothing more than is currently done toward instituting the educational reforms necessary to improve achievement. Standardized tests do not cause reform; they only cause finger pointing.

Standardized tests are only estimates of student achievement in broad curricular areas. They are not diagnostic measures of problems in the instructional processes. Standardized tests do not reveal how to reform education. In some significant ways they actually prevent reform, instructional improvement, and better learning.

The lock-step based norms that the test makers develop have insidious consequences. They are based on the chronological nine-month increments of the K–12 curriculum. The evils of the lock-step curriculum have been emphasized throughout this book. We feel that it is a major obstacle to educational reform. By making all normative indexes based on K–12 organizations, the tests confirm and preserve this structure. They require the organization because the numerical indexes would have no meaning without it.

In order to elevate performance on standardized tests within the lock-step, several practices appear to occur with considerable frequency. Failing students are retained to keep their lower test scores from affecting the scores of their chronological age peers. More special education students are separated from their non-handicapped peers for the same reason. By various strategies lower-achieving students are simply exempted from taking achievement tests.

Accountability and instructional improvement should result from testing. However, it must be conducted with the implicit purpose of doing this. It also must become part of the instructional process.

The effect of a particular teacher's instruction on the achievement of her or his students can be measured with standardized tests. First, a judgment should be made when selecting such tests about its content validity. Does the test appear to sample the general curriculum in use? If it seems to be a reasonable reflection of curricular content and its items are unambiguous as indicated by its stated reliability, then the test could be used as a reasonable estimate of achievement for a group of students.

The effect of instruction can be measured with such tests by assessing the students' achievement at the point of entry and exit. Teachers who have low-achieving and disadvantaged students should not be evaluated by comparing the performance of their students with that of more advantaged, higher-achieving students at the point of exit. The effect of instruction should be measured by comparing test performance at the beginning of the year with their performance at its close. Accountability is not served by judging performance other than on the same students over the instructional period. Where a particular group of students were when they arrived in a teacher's room and what the achievement increase during their stay was are the issues of accountability.

These are crude measures of achievement. Norm-referenced tests tell very little of particular accomplishments. However, the direction and increment of change in achievement can speak loudly on the quality of instruction. Students who make no measurable progress over a year with a teacher (or worse, actually decline) need protection from such inadequate instruction, and such teachers need help, training, or dismissal.

Positive changes in achievement can be more difficult to interpret but are to be applauded. Groups of students who are lower achievers to begin with may make more modest amounts of progress than those who are high achievers and rapid learners. It must be kept in mind that the interpretation of achievement scores is only useful and meaningful when the entry level, or baseline performance, of the students is known.

Some handicapped learners may require much more sensitive tests—tests that measure more and smaller increments of progress in order to detect the progress that might otherwise be overlooked. Again, sensitivity of the test and its appropriateness for a given group of students must be determined at an entry point. Otherwise, the post-testing really has no meaningful interpretation.

Knowledge at the beginning and end of an instructional period is necessary for judging how much achievement has changed. It is quite probable that the relatively high achievement of a group of able students at the end of a school year would be interpreted as good, unless it had been noted that there was no significant difference in achievement from the point at which they started the year. Teachers should be accountable for the achievement of their students, but the measurement of achievement for accountability must consider, first and foremost, the level of achievement of the students in their charge at the beginning of the instructional period. Only then can any reasonable judgment be made concerning how well teachers are discharging their duties.

When comparisons are made only against norms at the end of instructional periods, there will not be any useful measure of the achievement of the students under a particular teacher's care. This may cause teachers to avoid teaching classes comprised of lower-achieving students or particular students if their performance is likely to fall below the normative averages.

Lower-achieving and disadvantaged students can be protected by judging progress given their entering achievement level, then checking the amount of learning added by measuring achievement at the end of the instructional period. If teachers were judged by the value added rather than by normative comparisons, there would be little risk involved in their being assigned to groups of lower-achieving students.

Normative comparisons are interesting and occasionally useful, but these comparisons are for larger groups of students, schools, districts, states, or nations.

Teachers need to feel obligated to start teaching children at the achievement levels they have when they arrive in their rooms. When they understand that they are accountable for growth from these variable points, not some normative average, truly individualized instruction can occur. When teachers are held accountable based on norms, they are tempted, and often succumb, to teaching the specific items on a test or providing the answers so as to increase the scores. No good comes from such negative practice, and no good comes from putting teachers in the position where they are so tempted.

Substantive Assessment

Substantive assessment contrasts with normative assessment. Normative assessment produces abstract indexes which permit comparisons. Norm-referenced tests permit comparisons among groups taking the same tests. Substantive assessment attends to the specifics of what students know or can do.

Substantive assessment should encourage more substantive teaching.

As skills are acquired, they are listed in the credit column. If a curricular area has a skills hierarchy, then the curriculum itself can be used as a checklist. If the curricular area does not lend itself to the statement of clearly defined subskills, then substantive assessment can be made up of work samples. Samples can be taken from the entry point and at points along the instructional period. The samples taken at the end point of the instructional period indicate the current performance ability. The samples taken along the way mark the stages of progress.

These samples can be maintained in a portfolio, as would be the case with written composition, drafting, artwork, etc. It might be in the form of audio or video recording as in the case of speech in the language arts, speech therapy, or performance and motor activities.

A single project may take up an entire instructional period. The production of a play or the construction of a house takes long periods and incorporates many constituent steps. Observational information and feedback occur along the way, but the assessment is in the final product, the production of the play, the completed house. There will be many student participants whose individual contributions will need to be judged by the end product.

Narrative summaries of the students' contributions will be far more informative and useful than a grade. Also, when teachers are attending to and noting skill development along the way, useful feedback to the students is more likely to be incorporated in the learning activity.

There is current interest in moving toward substantive, performance-based assessment from norm-referenced standardized measures. We applaud the aim. We encourage the effort. We note that there is one very large obstacle in our educational system to implementing substantive, performance-based and authentic assessment procedures. This obstacle is our institutionalized system of grading students. More will be said on this topic in the next chapter.

Testing the Effect of Instruction

Tests should measure what was taught and in the same terms that it was taught. This is the essence of valid measurement, and for that matter valid teaching. We should be able to judge how well we are teaching with specificity.

We have dwelled on the importance of identifying and maintaining appropriate instructional levels as a fundamental assessment activity.

The instructional level at the beginning or entry point marks the baseline for achievement measurement. The instructional level at the end of the instructional period marks the achievement increase when it is compared to the baseline. The effect of instruction is the direction and magnitude of the difference between the two points. For students to achieve optimally, the instructional level should be maintained throughout. The instructional level is the most challenging level at which the student can experience success and task completion.

The instructional level in subject areas such as reading or math have rather well-defined instructional level guidelines. Areas which require physical performance (motor skills) must be broken down into subskills which are teachable units. For example, the sequence and complexity of learning to play a musical instrument must be graded in difficulty to make progress possible. The beginning gymnast must practice and master the simple exercises first in order to move on to the next more complex level which incorporates skills learned earlier.

Teaching these performance skills to most students requires that they be task-analyzed to make each step attainable for individually different students. The amount of practice needed to achieve mastery at each step will need to be varied, also.

The effect of instruction can be assessed in less direct ways. When students are provided appropriate instruction when given learning activities in which they can successfully engage, measurable changes occur other than in achievement. When children are permitted to be successful, school becomes a far more pleasant place to be. Improved attendance is the first measurable benefit of success-based assessment and instruction. Students who are permitted to succeed feel much better about school and they feel better about themselves. Schools that require success value students and the students implicitly understand this. Schools that respect students' need for success and self-esteem are in turn given loyalty and respect by the students. These benefits are measurable in the decline in vandalism and violence.

Instructional effort that is devoted to finding and maintaining success and continued progress for each student is rewarded by more time engaged in learning and less disruptive off-task behavior. Increases in engaged time and decreases in off-task and disruptive behaviors are measurable as well. These latter benefits may be the most significant for teachers. Dealing with off-task and disruptive behavior is demoralizing and time wasting. There is nothing more rewarding to a teacher than having students engaging in and completing schoolwork successfully. The conditions that produce these behaviors should be set in place as a matter of standard practice. The benefits are measurable.

Graduation rates or completion rates are also measurable effects of instruction. Numbers of students persisting in school, dropping out of school, and finally completing school should be measured as a routine matter.

What happens to students outside of school and what happens after they complete or leave school should be evaluated, also. Schools should have some obligation to preparing students for life. How well it is done is measurable. There are some educators who feel that agencies other than schools are responsible for helping students live healthy and independent lives. We feel that this is an obligation that schools no longer have a choice in making. The burden of the ultimate independence and welfare of many citizens has been placed on the schools by default. Schools cannot simply have one kind of curriculum, a "cognitive learning" curriculum. A free and appropriate education for all children requires diversity in curricular offering. The offering must serve the students' needs and society's needs as well.

Certainly, neither society's needs nor students' needs are being met when so large a segment of our population is unemployed, at odds with the law, and unhealthy. Our schools are being evaluated and blamed for what happens to students outside of school or after they leave school.

At least one-third of our students are not served well in regard to the essential life skills necessary for healthy, independent living. Our schools are evaluated in terms of these deficiencies, so such skills should receive prominent attention in the curriculum. One of the authors (Hargis, 1989) has proposed a curriculum which explicitly deals with these utilitarian areas. It is called the HOJE curriculum—the healthy, out-of-jail, and employed curriculum. It is not an entire curriculum, but it is the minimum standard which is expected for all students.

For the lowest-achieving and least advantaged students this curriculum may be challenging and require long-term effort to achieve. It is not considered a limit or a cap on students. Continuous progress at instructional levels is encouraged for all students through the highest achievement level in the most academic of curricula. However, the HOJE curriculum must be an added, but also an honored, curricular component that leads to independence and to a societal contribution.

One of the authors has prepared tests and curriculum guides, the

BRIGANCE® Inventory Of Life Skills (In Press) and the *BRIGANCE® Inventory of Workplace Skills* (In Preparation). Both of the tests and curriculum guides are designed for secondary programs to help teachers instruct and evaluate in these critically important curricular areas.

The ultimate assessment of the effects of instruction will be the statistics from the U.S. Departments of Labor and Human Services. The measures will be the employment figures, the crime statistics, incarceration rates, and infant mortality rates, among others. The lack of specific curricular attention to the basic life skills is a deficiency that causes chronic societal problems and is causing an enormous drain on our resources. The expense for incarcerating juveniles and adults in various states ranges from about $26,000 to over $60,000 annually. The cost of building one secure cell ranges from about $80,000 to over $100,000, and many more are needed as the incarceration rate expands dramatically. This money could be far better spent in providing success-based and HOJE curricula in our schools. The effect of this instructional treatment would be most directly measured in a surplus of prison cells.

Chapter 9

GRADING

Grading comprises the foundation material as well as the structural fabric of the educational system in the United States. In most of our educational system students are graded far more than most agricultural and manufactured products. Like eggs, students are sorted and grouped, labeled and ranked, compared and rejected. This grading goes on all through their school careers. Grades form a good part of our educational culture. They are the frame of reference. Grades form our current educational paradigm, and this paradigm remains stable even when educational reform efforts are tried. This paradigm must shift.

Grades form the lock-step of our school organization, K–12. Children are first graded by chronological age. They are further graded and sorted within this system by various grouping or tracking practices. They are then graded on the basis of their performance in the lock-step curriculum as they progress through it. Those that don't fit or conform are recycled, reclassified, and often rejected.

Poor grades are generally viewed as a symptom of a variety of educational problems. We reject this view. We believe that our grades and grading practices are not symptoms but causes of many of our educational ills. These ills are caused by grades, no matter which way they are produced.

Normative grading systems, "grading on the curve," emerged early in this century (Hargis, 1990). In 1908, Meyer presented the system and the distribution of grades we think of today. Meyer's grading system put 50 percent of the students in the middle. He placed 22 percent in each category he called inferior and superior, and 3 percent in each category he called excellent and failures. In 1914 Florian Cajori presented the 7-24-38-24-7 distribution. He also presented a table for normalizing scores. This system appears to be the one most commonly viewed as grading on the curve today.

The introduction of the curve was an attempt to objectify grading and protect students from some of the problems posed by absolute grading systems. In this system, grades are assigned to percent scores at arbitrary points. For example:

- A: Excellent—93–100
- B: Good—85–92
- C: Average—77–84
- D: Below average—70–76
- F: Failure—0–69

Many teachers are required to grade on a percent system such as this. The position of each grade on the scale is usually established by the school system. Teachers are to keep cumulative accounts of scores for each student, and when grades are to be issued the scores will be compared to the standard and grades assigned. This will be done without regard to any distribution of scores. Even though a C can be called average, it is not an arithmetic average. It is only an arbitrary segment of the scale. It is possibly, even likely, that in a particular class a true mean of scores would be nowhere near the C range. The average score on a difficult test might be 55, for example. If the grading scale were rigidly applied, most of the students would fail. The "curve" was an attempt to protect students from such circumstances.

The grading systems that evolved often incorporate the 100-point scale and a five-point letter grade. Occasionally, a single cutoff pass-fail system is used with it. Again, the cutoff is arbitrarily placed.

Distribution of Scores

Whatever the system, normative or point scale, a range of scores is considered necessary and desirable. The prevailing view is that only a minority of students should do well. An A must mean something. Some students should fail. This also for the same reason. Most students should fall somewhere in between. We are in principle disagreement with this attitude.

A distribution of scores and grades will be induced any time a normally variable group of students is confronted with the non-variable, single curricular offering assigned to any grade and classroom. It is remarkable that we know beforehand that there will be a wide range of abilities in each classroom, and that the grades and scores will simply verify this fact. Somehow we block out this information and impose the lock-step curricular offering on the students, thereby producing the distribution of grades, and then we blame the students for poor performance.

Grades Require Failure

Students whose current achievement levels are sufficiently below the skill requirements of their grade will do very poorly. Usually the low skill is reading ability. More than one-quarter of the students in any grade grouping will be out of this tolerance limit in reading ability. They will receive the low and failing grades.

Having grades means that the whole range must be applied to the students. Further, there is pressure to make certain that some students get failing grades and that not too many students get very high grades. Teachers who seem too generous may be accused of contributing to grade inflation.

Failure marks the mismatch between student ability and curricular offering and grade placement. Students receiving the failing grades are most often casualties of the rigid lock-step. Failing grades are primary evidence that the system has failed to individualize instruction.

As imperfect as most standardized achievement tests are, they are still good evidence of the variability in achievement levels of students that arrive in classrooms each fall. Our grading system makes us disregard this information. Instead of attempting to provide levels of curriculum and instructional material that matches the actual range of ability levels, one level of instruction is provided and, of course, this will produce the distribution of grades that is unfortunately deemed desirable. However, we should remember that this distribution typically will only mirror the normal variability of the students.

Grades and Good Teaching

For some teachers, harsh grading standards are equated with good teaching. Some teachers actually take pride in giving few good grades and giving many poor ones. These teachers believe that high standards means harsh grading. This makes a truly distorted definition of the nature of good teaching.

Grading harshly means that the teachers are exceeding the instructional level needs of most of their students, certainly for those who are given poor and failing grades. Only those few students who are able and competitive enough to attain the high grades will be rewarded in such an environment. The rest will be in a constant state of apprehension and demoralization.

Cheating

In such harsh, competitive classrooms, the temptation to cheat is great. Many students will realize that the only way open to them to keep from failing or to get a better grade is by cheating. Such harsh and competitive environments are not good for learning or achievement. Further, these classrooms do not model appropriate ethical or social behaviors or attitudes. Students are pitted against each other in competition for grades. There is no thought of helping or cooperating in such environments. When students are constantly admonished to do their own work, giving help would be interpreted as cheating. Most students leave such classrooms worse off than when they arrived, even if they are among the few fortunate ones to have received acceptable grades.

All students should do well as a matter of policy and practice. Students should be in an environment that encourages helping and cooperating. When everyone is supposed to do well and their orientation is that of helping their peers do well, cheating disappears as an issue.

Wasted Energy

Grading requires that much assessment effort be directed to that function. Teachers give tests so that they can determine grades to put on report cards.

Tests are given periodically during each grading period. The grade book requires a good many entries over a year's time. Daily work and homework will be scored and the results entered. Weekly tests may be given, scored, and entered. At the end of grading periods, when report cards are to be issued, final exams may be administered. All of this assessment effort is concentrated and distilled into a score or a letter. The scores and grades will be summed and divided to produce the final grade. The final grade will label the student's performance either comparatively with their peers or against the school's absolute standard. All of this potentially useful energy has been devoted to producing marks that have no instructionally useful function.

Assessment should be used to provide helpful feedback to students.

Scoring should be used to find what and how much students have or have not mastered so that instructional activity and material can be modified accordingly. Final summative evaluation should tell specifically what has been mastered and on what students are currently engaged. This is useful information for instruction, for transition to the next class or grade, and for students and their parents as well.

Negative Cumulative Effects

A student may do poorly at the beginning of a grading period but catch on and catch up by its end. The student's performance at the end may indicate mastery of the course objectives. However, the student's grade will not reflect this. The grade will include the early poor performance scores and will be pulled down by them. Grading practices take attention away from mastery of objectives. They can have a demoralizing effect when students know that no matter how well they may ultimately do, they must carry the early low score baggage with them to the very end.

The reverse of this situation can occur as well. Early high performance can decline. Passing grades can be awarded to students who have not mastered course objectives, when early high performance balances low, late performance. In either of the cases described above, what is lost sight of is actual learning. The end product of assessment does not reflect what has been learned.

Prevents Individualization

Grading requires that there be no real individualization of instruction. Some will claim instruction is being individualized, but when the levels of instructional difficulty being offered are narrowly limited to grade level, no legitimate individualization can occur. Attempts at individualization are usually directed at trying to help lower-achieving students get closer to grade level performance. Often, it is simply an attempt to help students with grade level assignments at which they are presently failing.

Often, individualized instruction is mistakenly thought to be one-to-one or very small group instruction, more individual attention. The real essence of individualized instruction is missed. The important feature of individualized instruction may have little to do with the ratio of students to teacher. It has very much to do with how well the match is made between the student and the level of instruction and curricular difficulty. Individualized instruction means that students are engaged in individually appropriate instructional level activities, and that their performance is at the success level.

Grades require that variable students be required to work at one or limited levels in order that a distribution of grades can result. Legitimate individualization cannot occur. The primary evidence that it has not will be a distribution of grades.

Shifting Blame

Grades permit us to shift the blame for failure to the student. We have a distribution of grades that must be assigned. Poor performance simply means that the student is not trying hard enough or there is something wrong with him or her. The blame certainly cannot be attributed to the fact that we are forcing the students into a lock-step curriculum where no real individualization occurs. It cannot be that poor and failing performance is evidence of the casualties of such a system.

Under the grading system, blame must be assigned along with the grades to the students. It will not be assigned to the true culprit, namely, the system of grading itself. Blame may also be assigned to the parents or lack thereof. It may be assigned to previous teachers who didn't prepare the students. It may be attributed to lack of resources or class overcrowding. Many of these things may contribute, but they seldom are as fundamentally implicated as is the grading system itself.

Entry Levels Not Identified

Failing grades are concrete evidence that the students receiving them are not at the correct instructional level on their curriculum. Poor performance and failing grades should be a signal that an appropriate entry level has not been identified and action should be taken to find a point of entry where failing performance can be changed to success. Unfortunately, since some failing grades are expected, no adjustment will be made in the instructional levels for the failing students.

Failure may even be required for an extended period before any action is taken. The action will often be retention at grade level or the repetition of courses at the secondary level. The student will be moved in lock-step in an attempt to fit or recycle him or her in the curricular lock-step. This will be done without regard to assessing whether or not it is at an appropriate instructional level entry point. The recycling is done without regard to whether or not the student has achieved a level of readiness which would permit success a second or even a third time around.

It is an unfortunate fact that students will be placed in grades or classes with the foreknowledge that they are in all probability going to fail.

Segregates Curricular Areas

A curriculum is neatly assigned to grade levels and courses. Individual curricular components are assigned to grading periods and finally apportioned to each of the 180 days of the school year. A teacher becomes the custodian of the portion of the curriculum assigned to him or her. The teaching that occurs is intended to dispense curriculum through instructional activities that are sequenced to fit the days in the school year. Instruction becomes curriculum centered. Students are in the room to receive the curricular dispensation. Their grades are merely the indicators of the extent to which they benefited. Grades are the indicators of the extent to which they are ready and able to start and keep pace with the dispensation.

We expect the distribution of grades. The distribution satisfies the need for giving grades and hence confirms the isolated lock-step structure of the curriculum. This system of grading insures that the curriculum is held in higher esteem than the students. It is the students' responsibility, not the responsibility of the schools, to insure that all students succeed. The curriculum remains isolated in grades and slots. The opportunity for continuous progress of all students who are out of tolerance is blocked.

The assessment system is used to determine student performance in the lock-step slots in the curriculum. If assessment were used appropriately, curriculum and its position would not be held in such inflexible lock-step positions. Curriculum would be assigned to individual students.

The first step in assessment is preventing failure. This is done by finding current level of achievement or functioning. Curriculum is matched to this. The routine assessment that follows is to make sure that success is maintained and that progress is continuous. Conventional grades are not possible in such a system. Substantive reports of progress are.

The curriculum cannot be segregated in lock-step slots if we want to prevent casualties and to produce continuous progress in all students.

Spawns Specialists

In order to dispense curriculum in lock-step slots, specialists in that curricular content are required. Specialists may learn much about the content that they are required to dispense. They may learn a variety of different ways of dispensing the content, but the content itself reigns supreme.

There are some superficially appealing features of the specialist system. Some feel that teachers are more skilled and interested in limited curricular areas. There has even been some interest in moving the specialist system down to the elementary grades. However, we feel that teachers should be ready to handle instructional levels that inevitably vary widely both below and above the specialists' slots. The specialists develops proprietary feelings toward the curriculum in their charge. They do not feel the same obligation for their students.

Students that fail in the specialist system are assigned the fault for their failure. The specialist is above suspicion. Poor performance on the part of the students is only evidence of how well the specialists are guarding their curricular domain. If students are doing poor and failing work, then they need more specialists to find out what is wrong with them and then still more specialists to provide the remedial intervention that such diagnosis reveals. School psychologists, special reading teachers, special education teachers; the specialist system breeds more specialists to deal with the consequences of the system itself.

Highly developed skills and knowledge in subject areas is desirable, but it is not more important than knowledge of assessment procedures that engage students at appropriate instructional levels and insure student success. These latter skills are far and away the most important for a teacher to have.

Grades Prevent Authentic Assessment

Grades, in many respects, call attention away from the subject of what has been and is being taught to how students are doing compared to others or to grade level standards in general subject areas without respect to any specific curricular content. Grades are abstract and normative. They provide an effective screen between the public and the curriculum.

Authentic assessment, on the other hand, is reported in terms of the content itself. There is no concealing or obfuscating that which constitutes the curriculum. Authentic assessment reports achievement in terms of what specific items on a curriculum have been learned. Moreover, samples of the work performed are to be included as often as possible.

Grades, unfortunately, have become such an institutional part of our educational system that they have taken on almost more substance than curriculum content itself.

Working for Grades

Since grades have taken on so much substance, they have become the end product or goal for much student effort in school. Learning has become secondary to the all-important grade.

Much student time is devoted to trying to figure out how a teacher is going to construct a test and what teachers want in the way of answers. How to get a good or passing grade is the focus of study time. It takes the place of the motive to learn. Grades cause this gross distortion away from learning.

Grades place students in competitive isolation from each other when the number of good grades is limited. Effort is changed from attaining objectives to attaining grades, and, since the tests and curriculum are the same for all students in the room, the less able and competitive students will be frustrated and demoralized.

Are Grades Motivating?

To the extent that fear can motivate, grades motivate some students. Students who are reasonably able will study enough to get passing grades. Students who are less able can only get a passing grade by cheating and are often motivated to do so. Students who want a higher grade than they can obtain in the lock-step will be motivated to cheat in order to get a higher grade. The only students who seem really motivated by grades are those who are already able to get them (Evans, 1976).

Some teachers may even use grades to control or punish. It is possible that students may have learned quite a lot, but their attendance, behavior, or "attitude" has irritated the teacher and the grade reflects this rather than learning.

We feel that assessment should focus on the substance of what has been learned and the setting of reasonable attainable objectives that students can engage in learning successfully. The reports of performance should be authentic and substantive. Grades have no place under these conditions.

Chapter 10

SUCCESS-BASED ASSESSMENT AND SCHOOL ORGANIZATION

Success-based assessment requires that a curriculum be offered on a flexible continuum which permits individual students to proceed along its path at widely varying rates. It should also have different options that lead to independence and productivity. Our current lock-step school organization works against implementing a success-based assessment system. Our current assessment practices foster the continuation of our lock-step school organization.

In order to see how school organization should be modified to insure success, we will first review standards used to structure our current school organizations and the problems these standards and organization cause.

Standards and Norms

Norms have grown out of our desire for standards and standardization. We have seen the benefits of standards. Standards of various kinds touch virtually all aspects of modern life. Even though standards are pervasive, many are outside our conscious awareness. Legal codes, construction and manufacturing codes are such. There are multitudes of professional, trade, and manufacturing associations that determine and define standards. We have a bureau of standards to organize and keep track of the myriad of standards used in measurement and production. Organizations such as Underwriters Laboratories are devoted to testing products to see if they conform to standards.

When we buy replacement parts for our cars we expect them to fit exactly. When we purchase standard cassette tapes, regardless of brand name, we expect them to work in our, or any other, cassette player, without regard to manufacturer. Interchangeability is an important part of standardization in the manufacturing process. It made mass production possible. Mass production has been of great benefit in the production of consumer goods, but it has its dark side, particularly when the technique is applied in mass education.

The application of mass production techniques to mass education was and is an appealing notion. The industrialization of the country coincided with the institution of mass free public education. Millions of students needed to pass through the pedagogical manufacturing process. However, there is one problem in education that resists the solution used in industry. This is the problem of tolerance limits. Variation in shape and dimension need be kept quite small in manufacturing. This is possible with machine-made parts. We often think of interchangeable parts as being identical. In fact, they do vary from each other somewhat. However, if they vary too much, they won't fit; they fall outside the tolerance limits. When items being assembled are within tolerance limits, the manufacturing process is smooth and the end product performs correctly.

Tolerance limits define the amount a part can vary from the standard and still fit and function. We can measure and control tolerance limits far better for machines than we can for humans. Humans vary widely on their various dimensions, but they must fit into a variety of structures and machines, all of which were designed and constructed according to standards. Engineers have done much to fit these devices and structures to humans. The standards used in building codes, for example, consider height and width of door frames, height and depth of stair steps, and the height and depth of countertops and cabinets. A single measure is often the standard for each of these.

Standards are set at tolerance levels that accept the majority of the normal range of human sizes. For example, the minimum door height for residential doors is six feet, eight inches. This will provide a sufficiently high opening for most individuals. However, consider the normal variation in human height. The word *normal* must be emphasized. People may be abnormally tall or short due to genetic or biochemical disorders. These disorders produce height outside the normal range. Still, the normal range of height extends from about four feet, six inches to about seven feet, six inches. Certainly, the extremes of this range are infrequent but exist. Everyone up to about six feet, six inches can use these doorways without apprehension or caution. The tolerance limit is generous, but it still handicaps a small, but normal portion of the population.

How do people at the other end of the height continuum cope with standards? Consider, for example, the standards for kitchen counters and cabinets. Anyone who is shorter than about five feet, three inches will be handicapped. They do not have the height to reach items in most of the cabinets.

Consider the fate of the 4-foot, 11-inch police cadet in Baltimore who completed basic training but failed the course when she couldn't reach the gas or brake pedals in the police cruiser during the driving test (*Associated Press,* Wednesday, May 27, 1992). The law prohibits discriminating on the basis of height, but passing the driving test is mandatory.

Most individuals fit within the tolerance limits posed by most standardized items. However, a significant number don't, and they experience the inconvenience and discomfort of being out of tolerance on some dimension. The idea is absurd that people should be physically altered in some way to fit a standard. However, it is quite evident that we attempt to alter children to fit the standards imposed by school curricula.

A curriculum has been likened to a Procrustean bed (Hargis, 1987). We push and squeeze and try in various ways to force individuals to fit, but we only succeed in producing damage and casualties. If the students don't fit the tolerance range of the curriculum, they will be failing to achieve and then dropping out. They are casualties of Procrustean methods of dealing with students who are out of tolerance with curriculum standards.

How much variability is there in the students in each grade? How much tolerance does the curriculum have for this variability? The facts are clear: students are remarkably variable and schools have limited tolerance.

Chronological age is the only variable that is routinely considered. Most school systems have age-of-admission criteria for beginning kindergarten or first grade. Some schools require students to be six years old by July of the year in which they start school, while others will admit students whose birthday falls sometime in November. The four- or five-month range can make a significant difference in the maturity and school readiness of a six-year-old.

The earlier the admission date, the older and more mature the students will be, and the more likely will be the normal achievement of the younger students. However, the older students could be nearly seven when they begin first grade. If readiness correlated only with chronological age, teachers could likely handle the differences in their primary-age children in each grade of the lock-step. As Spache (1976) pointed out, teachers can cope with about six months variation in academic ability from grade placement. The problem is that chronological age correlates rather weakly with readiness and achievement. The actual variation in each grade is far more than a plus or minus six months. Readiness varies with substantial independence of chronological age. The actual variation in attained reading achievement in first graders in the United States exceeds three years, more than a plus or minus 18 months. The variation increases at each subsequent grade by about a year.

Chronological age grouping gives the misleading impression that variability is much more restricted. On average, the variation in chronological age remains about the same at each grade level: about a year. This should not be used as the rationale for the single level of instruction provided at each grade.

The Curriculum

Curriculum is the aggregate of topics that make up the course of study in a school. All of the content areas that make up the course of study in our schools must be tailored to accommodate the school calendar. The scope and sequence of skills and topics must fit within the twelve or thirteen (1–12 or K–12) nine-month increments. Only a certain amount of time is allotted for each topic before moving on to the next. Those topics assigned to each grade must be covered before the year is over. This must be done so that the students will be ready to continue on the curricular sequence the following year. The curricular content advances in difficulty, but it advances in lock-step. The grid that it forms as it is fitted with the school calendar compels students to progress through it in lock-step. Each school year is further subdivided in smaller units. School systems differ considerably, but generally the divisions are marked by testing and grading. The curriculum has very large and very small lock-steps.

The curricular items assigned to each lock-step have been placed there by a normative trial-and-error process covering many years. The curricular demands of each level must be reasonable for most of the students who survive to reach the next grade.

The level of difficulty and the rate of progression must have a threshold of difficulty that permits the majority of students to proceed along the curricular path. The threshold must be low enough for the majority of students to achieve. As a consequence, it is below the skill level of the high-achieving students. High-achieving students are required to pace themselves at the lock-step rate of their age and grade peers. Unfortunate are the lower-achieving students who fall below the threshold of their assigned lock-step. The most direct, and problematic, approach to dealing with students that fall outside the threshold of their lock-step grade placement is either acceleration or deceleration. In the latter case it is referred to as grade retention; in the former, grade skipping. In either case, it will be done within the lock-step.

The curriculum, unfortunately, is assigned to the grade and calendar sequence and not to individual students. Each student's inherent pace of learning should instead dictate what curricular item to start working on and the length of time spent mastering it. A curriculum should be assigned to students for them to work through at their own pace. Curricula should not be assigned to grades; this practice reinforces the lock-step and produces casualties among the students who are out of tolerance with it.

The lock-step organization of our curriculum within our schools is firmly institutionalized. There are several conservative influences that prevent change in the lock-step curriculum. Once it was held that students would stay in the lock-step as long as they could benefit, and then it was expected that they would leave school.

Commercial curricula emerged to assist students who were headed to clerical jobs in business. Vocational training in skilled crafts was for the most part handled outside of school through apprenticeships. Students often left school to seek this training on the job or enter military service.

Mandatory attendance laws changed the order of things greatly. Schools were compelled to develop less academic curricula and tracks. Vocational offerings increased. Some special education programs for the "educable" mentally retarded were started. However, even with the attempts to find a place for more students, the new tracks developed simply formed new lock-step sequences.

Tracking and grouping procedures with mandatory attendance laws did increase enormously the number of students who completed school. The number completing high school reached 20 percent by 1940, just over 50 percent by 1953, about 67 percent by 1965 (Kronick and Hargis, 1990). Various compensatory programs were added to the schools in the 1960s and 70s. These programs further reduce attrition rates somewhat, but these programs are designed to help students fit lock-step structures. Still, about three or four students per classroom are failing at the elementary grade levels, many more are doing poorly, and about 20 to 30 percent of high school students drop out.

Conserving and reinforcing lock-step structures in our curricula is the industry that produces instructional materials. Commercial instructional materials are designed to fit existing curricular structures. If the material didn't fit some lock-step slot, it wouldn't sell. Commercial material fills the time devoted to its subject matter each day throughout the school year. These materials provide lesson plans and instructional activities for teachers. Some teachers become so dependent on these materials that they expect students to acquire most of their learning from the materials rather than use the materials to facilitate the teaching and learning process.

Most students make reasonable progress through schools using these commercial materials. However, these programs are rigidly lock-step in design. They have tolerance limits. If students enter a grade with readiness levels below that required to use the material, they will do poor and failing work. Students below the tolerance threshold quickly lose motivation and go off task. Consider the following example to illustrate these points.

A seventh grade science teacher is responsible for teaching 150 students in five classes each day. All classes use the textbook designated for this grade. We know from the last achievement test results that fully one-fourth of these students are performing significantly below the seventh grade level. Informal assessment of the students while they attempt to read and comprehend the material confirms that it is far too difficult for many to engage in effectively. These students are not willingly doing poor work; they are just out of tolerance with the instructional level provided by the commercial material.

The lock-step form of the curriculum and materials provide a cap on the achievement of the higher-achieving members of this seventh grade group. Achievement well above the seventh grade level in seventh grade students is to be expected and can be verified from the normative data on standardized achievement tests. These students will be out of tolerance with the instructional level along with their lower-achieving peers, though they may not share the painful circumstances. Nonetheless, a good many high-achieving students will chafe at the tolerance limits imposed upon them.

It is an unfortunate artifact of the lock-step that the instructional offering at each step may very well be a cap on the performance of a good many students. It is worse for the lower-achieving group, however. Poor and failing performance means that the instructional offering cannot be engaged in, and the students must fall farther and farther behind.

So many students perform adequately in the lock-step that we get the misguided notion that all students should perform at least adequately. If they don't, we make the assumption that something is wrong with the students; they are defective in some way. If they don't keep pace they will be retained, repeat a lock-step in its entirety. As they fall far enough behind their potential we may conclude that they are learning disabled. We almost never conclude that the majority of students with learning problems are out of tolerance with the lock-step curriculum and have become its casualties.

All students must conform to curriculum and grade structures. The extent that they fit their assigned structure is often reflected by the distribution of grades given to them. We almost never think of viewing the distribution of grades as an assessment of how well students fit their lock-step slot. We view poor grades as a student problem. When students do poorly long enough we are prepared with batteries of other tests that are aimed at finding defects in students and in providing a label that we use to place the student with others who share the same problem. This is the special education track.

Specialist Teachers

Teachers also fit, serve, and perpetuate the lock-step structure of our schools. Teachers specialize in teaching specific grades or subjects. Teachers specialize to fit slots in the curriculum. Teacher training programs and teacher certification standards emphasize such specialization. Teachers of necessity become responsible for particular sets of curricular items that fit their place in the lock-step system.

The objective of instruction is to get the materials presented. This instruction is curriculum centered rather than student centered. The educational structure focuses on the importance of presenting all of the material assigned to the grade or course so that students completing it will be ready for the next curricular lock-step. The system is indifferent to the fact that some students are not keeping pace. The pace of presenting the curriculum must continue.

The actual range of achievement of students in any grade extends to grade levels well below and well above their grade. This is an indisputable fact. Still specialists tend to avoid conceding that this variation exists or view it as defects among the students or as the result of inadequate teaching by some previous specialist teacher.

The mind-set of specialists is so dominated by the portion of the curriculum in their charge that instruction seldom deviates from the plan for the year. Efforts at dealing with individual differences will be in modifying the mode of presenting the curriculum content, not at modifying the pace or level of difficulty for individual students. The content may be packaged in different styles, media, or technology, but it will invariably be the same curriculum.

The extent to which students' achievement matches the difficulty level of the curriculum offering will be reflected by the range of grades or scores student receive while laboring in it. The number of poor and failing grades is a clear measure of the mismatch.

The specialist system breeds still more specialists. When it was found that unacceptably large numbers of students in each age group could not keep up, grouping and tracking procedures were developed, with more specialists assigned to handle the alternative curricula. Still, one level of instruction within each group left unacceptably large numbers of students out of tolerance and failing. These curriculum casualties obviously would require still more specialized attention. Special education emerged to handle the new tracks.

This emerging brought the emerging of more specialists such as school psychologists, diagnosticians and learning disability specialists. Special education itself has undergone considerable subcategorization into specialty areas as it was discovered that there were still many students who seemed not to fit the developing slots.

Specialists are accountable only for their specialty. If some students are not benefiting from their particular service, then the problem should obviously be referred to another specialist. The referral process can become circular and unresolved if none of the specialists seem able to provide an effective service. If enough students remain without finding a place, a new specialist will emerge. Specialists are created to cope with problems caused by the specialist system.

Subject Area Specialists

Subject matter is organized for specialist teachers. Specialists are concerned with the content of the curriculum in their subject or grade.

They are isolated from other teachers and subject areas. Consequently, they are seldom aware of the general demands that other teachers place on students. They may develop unrealistic notions about the importance of the subject matter in their area.

Being specialists, they are not likely to integrate other subject areas or skills in their course content. When students don't have sufficient skill or background for specialists' subjects or grades, they will be unlikely to do much about it.

At intermediate and secondary levels, the teachers will see so many different students per day (150 or more) that they will not have time to evaluate the problems students have with their assignments, let alone provide any helpful feedback. They will have barely enough time to check assignments in order to give grades. The responsibility for learning in the specialist system shifts to the students. When students don't acquire the information or skills presented, it is the students' fault, not the specialists.

Alternatively, blame is shifted to other specialists. If students are doing poorly in a specialist's room, it will be because the students have been ill prepared. In either case it will rarely occur to the specialist to adjust the level of instruction to match the entry level skills of the students. The notion, in fact, is abhorrent to many specialist teachers.

All too often we have heard teachers accurately predict which among their students are likely to fail as they move to the next grade or class. Even with this foreknowledge of students' skill levels, specialist teachers willingly let them fail rather than adjust the level of curricular difficulty to match student needs so that they might succeed and achieve. The curricular domain of the specialist must remain inviolable.

Teachers will, in all likelihood, never encounter a classroom full of students who are so well grouped that their achievement levels and instructional needs are as similar as the instruction the teachers are prepared to provide. When teachers direct their instruction, it is to the norm of their instructional slot. Their instruction will hit the mark for those students who are in the normative target area, but it will miss those students who are functioning outside this limited target area.

Ultimately, there needs to be specialization. Training for careers and professions becomes increasingly technical. Our complex world requires specialization. However, for the K–12 curriculum, it is important for teachers to be familiar with and capable of teaching large sections of the curriculum. Every teacher needs to have the resources to teach students at the wide range of readiness levels they have attained when they arrive at that teacher's room.

Teachers with special skills should serve as resources in collaborative arrangements with other teachers. Teachers with advanced skill in any area should serve as collaborative resources for academically talented students who are functioning well above the level of the normative curricular offering.

Specialist teachers are the center of instruction. Rather than content-centered specialists, we should have student-centered teachers. We need teachers who specialize in producing continuous achievement progress in every student, not just in those in the normative target area. In this model of teaching, the student must be engaged in learning. The teacher needs to be more a monitor, mentor, manager and not a dispenser-performer.

Far too many students march through the specialist teachers' classrooms each day. It is extremely difficult to make instruction student centered when large numbers of students shift through period by period. It would be far better to have a single class of fifty students for the entire day than to have 150, thirty at a time. Teachers should teach a wider range of subjects, the content of which should be integrated, and thereby see many fewer students. The opportunity to integrate subject matter, particularly with the language arts, is greater, and far more attention can be given to planning for individual needs. The time during the day need not be divided by periods and bells. It can be used with greater flexibility and every student need not move in the same lock-step time schedule.

The specialist system makes accountability difficult to focus. It is difficult to focus because it is very easy to shift blame for lack of achievement. There are many convenient scapegoats to be found in the specialist system. The first group of scapegoats is made up of the students themselves. If they are performing poorly it is because they are not working hard enough. They don't pay attention, and they don't do their homework. They are lazy and lack discipline. Alternatively, we assume learning disabilities, and after enough time passes without progress students may, in fact, qualify for the label. The system cannot accept the fact that the students are casualties of the lock-step curriculum. There must be some sort of defect in them.

If the students aren't selected as the scapegoat, then their parents may be. The decline in family values, working mothers, single-parent families, disinterest in achievement, no supervision at home—these are among the many negatives attributed to the family. The social and cultural circumstances of the students and their families will be the target for blame. Poverty and language differences are also frequently cited.

Teachers can further transfer blame to other specialists in the system. There will be administrators, supervisors, school psychologists, special educators, special reading teachers—each of whom has an assigned territory. These specialists in turn can point the finger of blame to each other. There is an impressive array of targets for finger pointing. Administrators are allusive targets. They can shift blame to lack of support, plant, and resources. Culpability is never established. Fingers are pointed in every direction. Because of the abundance of scapegoats, we fail to see that the culprit is the lock-step system itself.

Testing

Most educational testing seems to be used for classifying, grading, and labeling. Most testing currently provides very little information that can be used in instruction. Testing is almost always completely separated from instruction and is an intrusive activity.

Most testing is normative in nature. Instructionally useful testing must instead be substantive. It should focus on what and how much is being learned. It should not be intrusive; it should be an inseparable, intrinsic part of instructional activity. Instead of being used to determine where students perform relative to their chronological age peers, it should be used to find each student's instructional level so that all students can succeed.

Instead of providing a metric that simply shows where specific students perform relative to others or relative to a standard, assessment procedures should provide a stable success metric that guides instruction. All students should do well. Assessment procedures should be used that monitor instructional activity so as to adjust it to produce the indexes that indicate success.

Our current normative testing methods compliment and foster the lock-step curriculum. In fact, norms, scores, percentiles, and grades are all based on chronological age and grade groupings. Given a standard set of test items, we measure how students perform relative to others in their normative lock-step slot. Given the single level of instruction offered in a classroom, the range of grades shows how much individual students learn compared to others in the room.

The primary purpose of norm-referenced testing is numerical description (Deno, 1989). When these tests are administered, variation in performance is produced, and the ordinal position of the score is used for classification, labeling, grading, or judging progress. The norms are established age and grade peer groups which are organized within the lock-step structure of our schools. In order that the numerical products of these tests mean anything requires the continuation the lock-step structure.

The product of most teacher-conducted assessment, grades, also requires the perpetuation of the lock-step organization. Only with the single level of instruction assigned to the grade slot can a distribution of grades be produced. If instruction were organized around the needs of individual students, the performance levels of the students would all be in the same range and no distribution of grades would be possible. The grading system further prevents individualization within lock-step structures. We get the notion that it is not fair to give different levels of work; if we did it would only produce grade inflation.

Currently, too much testing provides very little information that can be used in instruction. Too much of it is normative in nature and separated from instruction and is an intrusive activity. Testing should be an inseparable, intrinsic part of instructional activity. Instead of providing a metric that simply shows where specific students perform relative to others or relative to a standard, assessment procedures should provide a stable success metric that guides instruction.

Assessment procedures should be used that monitor instructional activity so as to adjust it to produce the indexes that indicate success.

Individual Differences

Our present methods of dealing with individual differences are far too often a waste of time and resources. The reason is that most effort is devoted to trying to make students fit lock-step curriculum standards. When students fail classes, for example, any special attention given to the students will be directed to helping them pass the classes they are failing. They may receive supplementary tutoring. Someone may read tests to those students with reading problems. All efforts will be on getting the student to conform in some way to the curricular standard.

The problem with most current procedures for dealing with individual differences is that they are designed to change the student to fit the curriculum, not the curriculum to fit the student. The curriculum must be made flexible enough to permit students to move along it successfully at their own paces. This is the essential character of individualized instruction. Our rigid mind-set, however, accepts the correctness of the lock-step curriculum. This mind-set perverts our efforts at dealing with individual differences to making students conform to the lock-step. In doing so, we are actually wasting resources and usually making things worse.

Many descriptions of individualized instruction have to do with class size and student-to-teacher ratios. The assumption is the smaller the numbers, the greater the individualization must be. Individualization can be done without regard to class size, and, in fact, it becomes more important the larger the classes become. The authors' experience with rural schools has shown that in large multi-age classrooms individualization of the curriculum is done as a necessary standard practice. Of course, however, fewer numbers of students makes observation, preparation, and instructional time more manageable.

The reduction in class size may be used as a rationale to make it possible to force all the students to work at one level. Teachers recognize that students in any classroom are diverse in their achievement levels. Consequently, they say that the only way they can make them all work at the same level is by reducing the number of students so they can better help them work at this single level. Here again we have perverted the effort at dealing with individual differences.

Some teachers believe that students require different instruction according to their individual learning style. They feel that students may prefer to learn through different sensory modalities, such as the auditory, visual, tactile, or kinesthetic. These teachers feel that students should be tested to determine their preference, and then teaching activities developed to emphasize the strength of individual students.

Again, even though attention is given to some individual characteristics, the actual instructional level needed to produce success is not the focus, only the perceptual format is. The results of such efforts at individualization, despite enthusiastic individual testimony, are disappointing (Powell, 1987). Clearly, the perceptual format of instruction must be altered if a student has a significant visual or hearing impairment. However, for non-handicapped students, the most important element of individualization is making the match between individual students and the instructional level of the teaching material and activities.

Curing individual differences as if they were a sort of malady seems to be the aim of much so-called individualized instruction. We resist accepting the fact that students vary in academic aptitude and interest. Our logic is truly defective when we conclude that all students should perform up to the average of their chronological age group. If we can't make all students equally able musicians, artists, athletes, or mechanics, how can we make them similar academically?

We should keep in mind the difference between normal and average. Average is a mathematical term that incorporates the entire range of levels. Normal is the total range of typical levels. Average is an abstraction. Very few students would actually fit at that precise level in any class on any skill. Normal is really a wide range of ability or aptitude levels.

The problem is not one of a discrepancy of a student's potential from the average of his or her grade. The problem that needs to be considered is the discrepancy between aptitude and achievement that emerges as a student fails. Keep in mind that students fail when they are not given work that is at their current instructional and achievement levels. Any proposed solution to our educational problems that is intended to make students conform to standards based on norms is not a solution at all. The solution to the problem is to adopt the practice of placing students at appropriate curricular levels where success and achievement may occur.

In summary, the lock-step curriculum, the specialist system, commercially prepared instructional materials, norm-referenced testing, and grading practices all work against producing genuine educational reform. We hold the erroneous presupposition that our current lock-step structure is correct. Much of what we use and do only supports our notion about it. In the next part of the chapter we will outline how success-based assessment procedures can lead to breaking down this presupposition and then to restructuring and reform.

A Different Type of Teacher—The Student-Centered Teacher

In Chapter 7 we outlined the essential features of success-based assessment. You will remember that success is its central focus. Success must be the central concern of instruction and in dealing with individual differences. Success is motivating, and it is also the main ingredient in learning. You must get correct answers in order to learn correct answers. Success is fundamental to achievement. The assessment procedure must lead the way. It must become part of all instructional activity.

This assessment system requires us to consider a different model for teaching and for the teacher. Teachers must be prepared to handle instruction on the curriculum at levels both well below and well above their specific grade. Students are actually performing years above and below their grade designation as a matter of normal occurrence. Remember, the range in reading achievement at the end of the first grade exceeds three years, and by the time this same group of students reaches high school age, this range exceeds nine years. Every unselected group of fourteen-year-old students have 5 percent or more reading at or below the fourth grade level. Twelve percent will be reading at or below the fifth grade level, and about 25 percent will be reading at or below the sixth grade level. At the higher-achieving end of this continuum, however, fully 22 percent of the students will have reached the ceiling measurement on many standardized tests; they will be reading at or above grade level 12.9! The standardization data available for norm-referenced achievement tests will confirm these figures. Local norms may vary by average performance, but the range in performance levels in fourteen-year-old students should be expected to exceed nine years.

Teachers need an array of instructional resources available to them to match these many ability levels. They need to be prepared to deal with many different curricular levels as well. In other words, the curriculum should be student centered. Just as the curriculum should be student centered, so should teaching. However, teaching today is not usually student-centered. It is usually devoted to the content of the curriculum assigned to the grade or course. Lectures, discussions, activities, readings, and assignments are prepared to cover the course content during the 180 days of the school year. Teachers may hope that a majority of students are engaged and making satisfactory progress. However, we know that this approach leaves out all those students who are out of tolerance limits, and teachers expect and accept the failure of a portion of their students.

Keeping students engaged in learning requires that the activities be at their own instructional levels. Students must be engaged more in the activities of the day than they are in the teacher-dominated lecture-discussion method. Instruction should be delivered according to what individual students can be engaged in and succeed in. The teacher's role in this system changes greatly. Matching instructional activities to students, selecting and preparing materials, and developing and monitoring activities take up much of the teachers' time.

Matching students with appropriate instructional level work requires that the teacher be constantly observing and assessing student performance in ongoing instructional activity and materials. Assessing and observing are fundamental to making the match and keeping students succeeding. Teachers must use the observed information to provide or adjust materials and activities matched to individuals to keep them at the success level. Teachers already do some observation and evaluation of student work, but it is for the purpose of giving students grades. With success-based assessment the focus changes entirely. The information gained from observation is used to evaluate the instructional match, not the student.

The activities outlined above should dominate teacher time. Students must be engaged. That is when they are learning, and that is when assessment information is obtained. Teachers appear to be only a participant in the daily activity. They will no longer be the principle player.

Classrooms must be well stocked and well organized to keep students engaged at a variety of individual instructional levels. It is possible to have each individual working independently with teacher supervision. However, there is ample evidence that mutual instructional activities including peer tutoring and cooperative learning have a substantial number of additional benefits. To make these systems work requires planning, organizational and management skill. Much of the teacher's time is devoted to managing, supervising, observing, and measuring. Materials preparation and selection takes a great deal of time with success-based assessment and instruction.

Success-based assessment is the system that should be used to keep students matched with instructional materials so that they succeed. Much teacher time needs to be devoted to observing student performance while they are engaged in learning activities. The teacher must also spend much time in supplying the curricular material that is used in the instruction/assessment cycle. Teachers are involved in instructional delivery, but they are not the dominating figure they are in the teacher-centered classroom.

Success-based assessment requires success-based instruction. Remember, instructional activity itself is used as the test in this system. Teachers monitor how well students are performing in the routines of learning to make sure that success and learning are ongoing. The instructional delivery system requires both cooperative learning activities and independent supervised study.

Too frequently, the teacher's evaluation is based on how a single level of content is presented. Teacher evaluation should place more emphasis on the teacher's skills for involving students in learning activities commensurate to their different skills and ability levels. This might include techniques such as cooperative learning, cross-age tutoring, supervised study, learning centers, etc., which allows each student to concentrate on material at their instructional level. The principle characteristic of a good teacher is the ability to manage instruction at all the different achievement levels of students. It is on this characteristic that teacher evaluation should pay most attention.

The principle characteristic of a good teacher is the ability to manage instruction at all the different achievement levels of any classroom full of students. It is on this characteristic that teacher evaluation should pay most attention. Smiley (1990) reports an incident in a student-centered, eighth-grade classroom that illustrates the conflict that occurs between the traditional and the proposed model of teacher evaluation. The students were enthusiastically engaged in a cooperative writing activity when the administrator in charge of teacher evaluation walked in the room. After a moment in the room she said loudly enough for all to hear, "I will come for the evaluation when you are teaching." This incident well illustrates the irony and the frustration that is produced by the conflict between the systems.

The amount of time students are engaged in learning increases. Consequently, the amount of material consumed is substantially increased. Topping (1988) states that the rate of progress and consumption of materials in peer tutoring and cooperative learning programs can cause embarrassment due to the speed at which the stock of available, relevant materials is exhausted.

Student-centered teaching is individualized in the sense that all students are engaged in activities that are at their own instructional levels. It might be compared to a model which existed out of necessity for many years—that used by resourceful teaching found in multi-graded school rooms in rural areas. No doubt many of these resourceful teachers felt they didn't have time to individualize instruction. However, in reality and of necessity, many of these teachers became masters at individualizing instruction.

The essential ingredient of real individualized instruction is that instructional activity is matched to the ability level of the students. The learning activity must be doable. The individualized match has been made when the students perform at the same level expected of adequately achieving students.

Instructional Delivery

Schools must have flexible curricula. It should range from life skill to academic. Its various levels should not be assigned to grades. Students should be permitted to emphasize one or the other and work their way through at the rate that insures success.

Teachers must be prepared to teach heterogenous groups of students. All teachers should be prepared to deal with basic skills and academic subject areas. Course work should not be tightly compartmentalized as it is in the conventional curriculum layout. Teachers should recognize that learning rates are diverse and uneven; curricular objectives should not be placed at the end of lock-step curriculum periods. These objectives are to be worked toward at whatever rate individual students can manage successfully. Most assessment should be in the form of observing or monitoring students actually engaged in learning activities and evaluating the actual products of this engagement.

This approach to instruction is not harder or more expensive than our current approaches. It is already commonly practiced in a variety of settings that don't receive much attention. We have already mentioned how the system is often practiced in many of the remaining rural schools.

In some very sparsely populated areas, instruction is delivered quite individually without the benefit of a classroom. One of the authors is personally acquainted with a teacher who delivered instruction by boat over a 1200-square-mile section of southern Alaska to larger groups of students than in typical classrooms. This teacher tried to meet with each student once a week, monitor progress, provide any needed assistance, and supply more instructional material. There were no grades given, instructional materials were matched to instructional levels, progress was continuous at many different levels, and there were no dropouts.

This is basically the model of teaching required for teachers of homebound or hospitalized students. The instructional material must be matched carefully to the students. They must be able to engage in its use fairly independently. Training in this system is what we recommend for all teachers.

Virtually all assessment effort must be devoted to adjusting instructional material to fit individual students. Grading no longer is the primary end product of most assessment. If this model is transplanted to schools and classrooms, additional benefits can accrue. Instructional material and current technologies can be concentrated there. Teachers can work in collaborative teams. Students can engage in cooperative, mutual instructional learning activities.

Classrooms that are organized this way cannot be governed by periods and bells. Curriculum cannot be assigned to grades; it must be assigned to students. Learning centers and learning resources that cover a range of curricular levels permit students to engage in learning for periods of time that extend to their need for success and mastery.

Because schools are organized by limited periods and bells, teachers rely on homework assignments to help students spend more time engaged in learning activities. However, teachers have come to rely on homework activities far too much. Homework has become one of the most abused and misused products of the lock-step curricular structure. Students who are able to engage in it get most of their engaged time from it. Those who are out of the tolerance limits of the course from which it is assigned do it poorly or not at all. No students should ever take work home that they cannot do accurately and successfully on their own. Homework, if it is given at all, should be for polish and fluency. The activities should be readily doable. There should be no opportunity to practice errors. Homework is no substitute for teaching in the classroom. Students should never take anything home that requires assistance that is not readily available to them.

Chapter 11

VISION AND HEARING

Vision and hearing problems, when severe, are readily detectable. Less severe, even marginal, problems with vision and hearing are not obvious and may go unnoticed. However, significant educational problems may result, and the real cause of the problem may be overlooked.

Educational assessment should include measurement of vision and hearing that sensitively attends to these mild and marginal problems. Vision and hearing screening should be routine as well as preliminary to other assessment. Screening tests are commonly given as a matter of school policy. Significant information can be gained from some of the screening devices.

Vision Screening

Ideally, vision screening will be supervised by a health professional. However, this screening can be conducted by the teacher, a paraprofessional or volunteer. The professional responsible for student health services should make provisions for:

- recording the screening results in the student's health record and do a follow-up screening, if warranted,
- following up with parental consultations and making referrals for services when the vision screening indicates these are needed.
- making arrangements for obtaining community resources which may be needed such as financial aid from organizations, such as the Lions Club, if parents cannot afford the needed services.
- consulting with the teacher on matters such as the findings and recommendations of the ophthalmologist.

When the services of a health professional are not available, the teacher is usually expected to assume some or all of the duties and responsibilities listed above. This may include conducting vision screening.

There are two components of visual function that are usually screened.

One is visual acuity and the other is binocular function (the use of both eyes simultaneously).

The best known and most widely used screening device for visual acuity is the Snellen test, named for a Dutch physician who developed it during the mid-nineteenth century. This test is the familiar chart composed of block capital letters in decreasing size starting at the top with a large letter E. The top line comprised of the single E is the 200-foot line. A person with normal vision should be able to discern this letter from a distance of 200 feet. Since the test is to be taken at a distance of 20 feet, if the only letter the testee can visually detect or read is the large E, then her visual acuity would be labeled as 20/200.

The test distance of 20 feet and the last line on which the majority of letters can be identified. If the last line successfully read is the 50-foot line, then visual acuity is labeled 20/50. So it goes until a subject identifies the letters on the 20-foot line and the acuity is described as 20/20. There are more lines below the 20 foot line, 15, 10, and 5. These numbers mean that persons with 20/20 vision would need to move up to 15 feet in order to read the 15-foot line, 10 feet to read the 10-foot line, and 5 feet to read the 5-foot line. A person who can read the 15-foot line from 20 feet would have visual acuity of 20/15, the 10-foot line from 20 feet would have an acuity of 20/10, etc.

The Snellen test measures only visual acuity for distant vision. It does not test visual acuity at the near point (distances at which most schoolwork occurs)—namely, the reading distance. The reading distance is approximately 16 to 20 inches. Further, the Snellen test measures visual acuity in each eye independently. Reading is normally a binocular activity whether at near point or distance. Other types of tests are required to measure binocular functions.

In regard to acuity as measured by the Snellen test, children are referred for further examination if they score 20/30 or less in primary grades and 20/40 or less thereafter. It is ironic that most of the children who are identified for referral will usually have no educational difficulties at all. It identifies children who are myopic (nearsighted). These children have excellent near point vision, 16 to 20 inches and even closer. This is the distance at which most schoolwork and reading is done. Even if the services of a health professional are available, the teacher has an important role to play regarding possible vision problems of students. The teacher is in a unique position to observe for vision problems which may not be detected by vision screening.

Also, if vision screening is only conducted annually, problems may develop between screenings. The observant teacher may be able to detect problems which develop between scheduled screenings and take the appropriate action.

The observant teacher is usually able to identify the students who are likely to have a myopic condition. This is especially true if the student is an avid reader. A student with a myopic condition can be observed as having the tendency to "put his head in the book" rather than keeping the reading material the normal or usual distance of about 15 inches from the eyes. This condition and observation tends to become more prevalent at about third grade age. Prior to this age, most children have greater accommodative power.

Accommodation is the process by which the muscles around the lens of the eyes change their shape in order to accommodate focusing on objects of various distances from the eyes. A loss of this accommodative power does not allow clear image of objects as the view changes over various distances. Eyeglasses may be needed to compensate for the eyes' loss of accommodative power.

In effect, students who are avid readers and do lots of near point activities are exercising their accommodative strengths in a narrow, close range. This may lead to a gradual loss of the accommodative power needed to focus on reading material at a greater distance, such as writing on the chalkboard. The student who has lost accommodative power may be observed squinting, blinking or straining as she attempts to change from focusing on near to distant objects. This squinting, blinking or straining is an attempt to overcome or compensate for the loss of accommodative power. Eyeglass lenses which aid in accommodating distant viewing may need to be prescribed.

Hyperopia, in terms of accommodation, is the opposite of myopia. This end of the acuity range can cause educational risk factors which may be overlooked. In fact, students who are hyperopic (farsighted) may not even be considered for referral. They are usually thought of as having unusually acute vision. It requires no effort to maintain a clear image at distance, but as the image draws closer, accommodative effort increases. Near distance work requires more accommodative effort for the hyperopic, while distance work requires effort for the myopic.

Accommodative powers in hyperopic individuals are typically maintained much longer than in the myopic. Interest in reading and normal achievement requires a good deal of accommodative exercise at near distances. Accommodative efficiency for near distance work is often retained by hyperopic individuals until middle age when reading glasses will be required.

Occasionally, students who are hyperopic may experience discomfort from extended accommodative effort at reading or doing other seatwork. If such students are, for a variety of reasons, having trouble with achievement, hyperopia can be a contributing factor to their learning problem. An effort should be made to balance near distance with far distance learning activities if there is any evidence of discomfort when doing seatwork.

Binocular Vision

Good vision requires that both eyes must work together in order for both to focus on an object with a clear image. There is actually a separate image from each eye transmitted to the brain. The muscles that move the eyes must move in unison and fixate precisely in order to produce a single well-focused image. If they do not, then two separate images will be transmitted to the brain (double vision). Good binocular vision, or good muscle balance, is required to produce a single image over the field and range of vision.

Most seatwork requires the reading of print from a distance of about 16 inches. In order to perform seatwork comfortably, the muscles which control each eye must work together to produce images which are transmitted to the brain as a blended or fused image. The eyes must be able to pull together toward the nose as objects come closer. Muscle balance and accommodation are measured in the way the eyes are aligned, as well as their flexibility in blending or fusing at near point.

The eyes must align on vertical and horizontal planes. If there is severe deviation (tropia), the alignment problems will be physically apparent and the eyes will look out of alignment. More severe muscle balance problems, surprisingly, are often of little educational significance. The vision in the non-dominant eye (the eye that deviates from the point of attention) will simply be suppressed. The person with the severe muscle balance problem will simply use one eye and no accommodation is required.

Any eye condition which requires undue strain on any eye muscle(s) may impede learning. This undue muscle strain may produce fatigue, making more difficult for the student to continue to perform seatwork for extended periods of time. The student, and teacher, are frequently not aware of the cause of this difficulty.

The potential for educational problems, ironically, may become greater as the muscle balance problems become less severe. The tendency (phoria) versus the severer manifestation (tropia) permits the student to accommodate with some effort. The effort can reach a stage of discomfort and distraction. The student can manage to focus clearly for short periods, but the eyes may involuntarily deviate as fatigue increases. Students may lose their place as repeated fixations are required as the eyes move rapidly over lines of print and make return sweeps to start new lines. Students may find each eye on different words or different lines as they lose accommodative function.

Some of these children will handle the problem unconsciously. They will simply start suppressing the image in one eye and use one eye to read. Other children may avoid near point work after a short time or appear to be inattentive or distractable. Probably the most helpful thing to be done for these children is to permit them more opportunity for distance work or larger format work. Keep the duration of activities within the threshold of their accommodative levels.

A point of emphasis is that vision screening should include measures of binocular vision at the reading distance. Schools often use devices that do this already. Instruments such as the Keystone Telebinocular and the Bausch and Lomb Orthorator are often available for screening purposes. They require individual testing, but they can be operated by volunteers, and they can be moved readily from school to school. They are often set up in mobile units. Another point of emphasis is that marginal binocular vision problems may have educational significance for some students. They should not be overlooked if a student is having trouble learning.

Hearing Screening

Hearing screening should be conducted or supervised by a well-trained professional, such as the audiologist or school nurse. Some speech and language specialists are well trained in conducting audiology screenings and evaluations. Using a portable pure-tone audiometer is a relatively simple task to perform. Paraprofessionals or volunteers can be trained to perform reliable pure-tone audiometer tests.

This testing must be individually and a prerequisite for obtaining reliable results is that it be conducted in a relatively quiet environment.

Usually three frequency pitch levels are sampled for testing. These frequencies are representative of the range required to perceive speech. If the screening test reveals a loss of 20 decibels or more in any one of the speech frequencies, a referral for an audiological evaluation is usually in order.

Following the screening the professional or assistant should:

- record the screening results in the student's health record and do a follow-up screening if warranted.
- follow-up with parent consultations and by making referrals for services the screening indicates are needed or in order.
- make arrangements for obtaining community resources which may be needed, including financial aid if parents cannot afford the needed services.
- consult with the teacher on matters such as findings and recommendations of medical professionals and clinics.

Hearing screening should be at least an annual event during the primary grades. Children who are transferring into a school should also be screened. The portable pure-tone audiometer is used for screening.

As with visions, the observant teacher is in a unique position to observe for possible hearing problems. Such observations should be followed up with a consultation with the appropriate person. Such consultation may include talking with the parents regarding observations and the possible need for an audiological examination.

The sensitive and observant teacher will observe for indications of hearing problems. These observations may include:

- asking that directions be repeated.
- not being able to join in a discussion effectively.
- confusion because of poor auditory discrimination (*top* for *stop*, *lift* for *left*, *in* for *end*, etc.).
- turning of the head to one side in order to favor the ear with the better hearing.
- a strained look on the student's face during activities requiring good listening skills.

Hearing Problems of Preschool and Primary Grade Children

The hard-of-hearing students are those with a hearing loss in the frequencies important for the perception and understanding of speech.

This means a loss of 20 to approximately 60 decibels in the 500 to 4000 Hz frequency range.

There are two variables that determine the extent of the problem that hearing loss causes. These are the extent of the hearing loss and the age of onset of the hearing loss. The interaction of these two variables causes a remarkably wide range of educationally related problems.

The rapid period of language acquisition that occurs from about 18 months until about age six is a particularly sensitive time for hearing loss to occur. If the loss occurs early in this period, the consequences are more profound. If the loss is present at birth or occurs before about age two, the loss is said to be prelingual and will have the most profound effect on language acquisition.

Children with relatively mild losses that have occurred prelingually or during early language acquisition often show evidence of this in lower verbal performance on intelligence and achievement tests. Misdiagnosis of mental retardation can result if there has not been hearing screening. Hearing screening should be considered prerequisite for the valid administration of intelligence or achievement tests. The commonly used intelligence tests are simply not valid instruments for use with children who have a hearing loss. There are nonverbal or performance tests available which can be used and interpreted by an experienced tester.

Hearing loss, especially during the preschool years, will cause various speech problems. Children model the speech that they hear. Hearing loss during speech development produces a range of articulation problems. Speech therapy is important to help with the articulation problems of these children, but it is equally important to help with the concomitant language problem that the hearing loss has likely caused as well.

Consequently and ideally, hearing screening should be a routine part of school admission. With conditions such as infections of the middle ear occurring more frequently during the primary grades, hearing screening should be conducted routinely during the primary grades. The observant teacher should observe for indications of conditions such as a middle ear infections and make the appropriate referral. Some hard-of-hearing students who have the ability to compensate for the loss manage to adjust and perform satisfactorily in school with relatively little assistance. Many students with a hearing loss who are identified as early and fitted adequately with a modern hearing aid can function remarkably well in the regular educational settings. Others will need much special assistance, which, unfortunately, is not always provided.

Children with severe hearing impairment are usually referred to special programs and receive special help. However, there is concern and reason to believe that many children who have milder hearing problems, but severe enough losses to cause learning problems, are neglected.

Census estimates of the number of school-age, hard-of-hearing students are scarce and uncertain. Estimates are that hard-of-hearing students outnumber deaf students about nine to one.

REFERENCES

Betts, E. A. (1946). *Foundations of reading instruction.* New York: American Book.
Brigance, A. H. (1983). *The Brigance Comprehensive Inventory of Basic Skills.* North Billerica, MA: Curriculum Associates.
Brigance, A. H. (in press). *Life skills inventory.* North Billerica, MA: Curriculum Associates.
Brigance, A. H. (in preparation). *Prevocational skills inventory.*
Commission of Reading. (1985). *Becoming a Nation of Readers: The Report of the Commission on Reading.* Washington: The National Institute of Education.
Deno, S. L. (1989). Curriculum-based measurement and special education services: A fundamental and direct relationship. In M. R. Shin (Ed.), *Curriculum-based measurement: Assessing Special Children.* New York: Guildord Press.
Ebel, R. L. & Frisbic, D. A. (1991). Essentials of educational measurement (5th ed.). Englewood Cliffs: Prentice Hall.
Evans, E. B. (1976). What research says about grading. In S. B. Simon & J. A. Ballanca, (Eds.). *Degrading the grading myths: A primer of alternatives to grades and marks* (pp. 30-50). Washington: Association for Supervision and Curriculum Development.
Gickling, E. E. & Thompson, V. (1985). A personal view of curriculum-based assessment. *Exceptional Children, 52,* 205-218.
Glasser, W. (1971). *The effect of school failure on the life of a child.* Washington: National Association of Elementary School Principals.
Grimes, L. (1981). Learned helplessness and attribution theory: Redefining children's learning problems. *Learning Disability Quarterly, 4,* 91-100.
Hargis, C. H. (in press). Success-based assessment. *Tennessee Education.*
Hargis, C. H. (1990). *Grades and grading practices.* Springfield: Charles C Thomas.
Hargis, C. H. (1989). *Teaching low achieving and disadvantaged students.* Springfield: Charles C Thomas.
Hargis, C. H. & Terhaar-Yonkers, M. (1989). Do grades cause learning disabilities? *Holistic Education Review, 2,* 14-18.
Hargis, C. H., Terhaar-Yonkers, M., Williams, P. C. & Reed, M. T. (1988). Repetition requirements for word recognition. *Journal of Reading, 31,* 320-327.
Hargis, C. H. (1987). *Curriculum based assessment: A primer.* Springfield: Charles C Thomas.
Hargis, C. H. (1982). *Teaching reading to handicapped children.* Denver: Love.
Jenkins, J. R. & Pany, O. (1978). Standardized achievement tests: How useful for special education? *Exceptional Children, 44,* 448-453.

Kim, K. S. (1991). *A comparison study of learning disabled and regular students' ability to self-diagnose words using a computerized curriculum-based assessment system.* Unpublished doctoral dissertation, The University of Tennessee, Knoxville.

Kronick, R. F. & Hargis, C. H. (1990). *Dropouts: Who drops out and why—and the recommended action.* Springfield: Charles C Thomas.

Lidz, C. S. (1981). *Improving Assessment of School Children.* San Francisco: Jossey-Bass Publishers.

Miller, G. A. (1956). The magical number seven, plus or minus two. *Psychological Review, 63,* 81–97.

Powell, L. C. (1987). *An investigation of the degree of academic achievement evidenced when third and fourth grade students are taught mathematics through selected learning styles.* Unpublished doctoral dissertation, The University of Tennessee, Knoxville.

Shinn, M. R. (Ed.). (1989). *Curriculum-Based Measurement: Assessing Special Children.* New York: The Guilford Press.

Shriner, J., & Salvia, J. (1988). Chronic noncorrespondence between elementary math curricula and arithmetic tests. *Exceptional Children, 55,* 240–248.

Simon, H. A. (1974). How big is a chunk? *Science, 183,* 482–488.

Smiley, F. M. (1990). Usable pasts and unlimited futures: A Discussion on selected tenets of whole language. *Holistic education review, 3,* 8–11.

Spache, G. D. (1976). *Investigating the issues of reading disabilities.* Boston: Allyn and Bacon.

Stanovick, K. E. (1986). Matthew effects in reading: Some consequences of individual differences in the acquisition of literacy. *Reading Research Quarterly, 21,* 360–407.

Starch, D. & Elliot, E. C. (1913). Reliability in grading work in mathematics. *School Review, 21,* 254–259.

Starch, D. & Elliot, E. C. (1912). Reliability of grading high school work in English. *School Review, 20,* 442–457.

Tucker, J. A. (1985). Curriculum-based assessment: An introduction. *Exceptional Children, 52,* 199–204.

Wittrock, M. C. (1991). Testing and recent research in cognition. In M. C. Wittrock and E. L. Baker (Eds.), *Testing and Cognition* (pp. 5–16). Englewood Cliffs: Prentice Hall.

Zigmond, N., Vallecorsa, A. & Silverman, R. (1983). *Assessment for Instructional Planning in Special Education.* Englewood Cliffs, NJ: Prentice-Hall, Inc.

INDEX

A

Accountability, 123–126, 150
Achievement, 17, 18
Achievement tests, 5, 46, 123, 133
Alignment of assessment and curriculum, 5, 6, 9, 13, 21
Attention deficits, 21, 63
Authentic assessment, 15, 24, 45, 56, 58, 87, 138–140
Automatic level, 121
Ayres Handwriting Scale, 59

B

Basal level, 60, 62, 82
Basic skills, 8, 13
Bausch and Lomb Orthorator, 164
Benchmarks, 12
Betts, E., 20, 31, 39–41
Binocular vision, 161, 163
Brigance Inventories, 51, 110, 112, 114, 116, 117, 120, 130
Busywork, 38

C

Cajori, F., 131
Cheating, 32, 134
Commission on Reading, 107, 108
Constructs, 14
Construct-referenced tests, 62, 63
Criterion-referenced tests, 45, 48, 50–52, 58, 105, 109–112
Curriculum, 3, 5, 6–8, 13, 14, 21, 23, 43, 48, 51, 79, 82, 89–91, 94, 103, 124, 125, 133, 137, 138, 144, 147, 155, 159
Curriculum-based assessment, 43, 53–56, 71, 72, 74, 81, 92, 105, 110
Curriculum-based measurement, 53–56
Curriculum casualty, 19, 20
Curriculum-referenced tests, 48, 53, 61, 69, 70, 73

D

Deno, S., 152
Diagnostic assessment, 17, 88, 90, 91
Discrepancy definition, 28
Double standard, 25, 26
Dropout, 29

E

Ebel, R., 71, 78
Elliot, E., 58, 67, 68
Engaged time, 21
Entry level, 61, 81–86, 88–90, 136, 137
Errors, 61
Error patterns, 31, 32, 104
Evans, E., 139
Exhaustive assessment, 103
Expectations, 26

F

Failure, 24–32, 34, 35, 42–44, 81, 85, 88, 89, 118, 133, 136, 137
Fluency, 33, 40, 107
Formative assessment, 51, 54
Frisbie, D., 71, 78
Frustration level, 20, 25, 31, 33, 40

G

Gickling, E., 71
Glasser, W., 49

Grades, 16, 22, 24, 31, 32, 35, 37, 44, 56, 59–61, 68, 86, 151
Grading, 30, 33, 131–140, 159
Grimes, L., 27

H

Hargis, C., 5, 9, 16, 17, 19, 20, 29, 33, 34, 49, 53, 68, 71, 72, 91, 129, 131, 145
Hearing screening, 164–166
HOJE curriculum, 129, 130
Hyperopia, 162, 163
Homework, 159

I

IEP, 103, 104
Independent level, 39, 100
Individual differences, 18, 35, 152, 154
Individualized instruction, 135, 136, 153, 157, 158
Informal assessment, 44, 59–61, 99, 105, 146
Instructional level, 20, 26, 34, 38–42, 55, 71, 84, 87–90, 127, 128, 153, 156
Intelligence tests, 19, 28, 93
Intrinsic assessment, 87
Item difficulty, 48

J

Jenkins, J., 47

K

Keystone Telebinocular, 164
Kim, K., 91, 92
Kronick, R., 16, 29, 145

L

Lake Wobegon Effect, 10, 11
Learning disability, 19, 20, 28, 29, 87, 90
Learning rates, 18, 19
Lock-step curriculum, 15–22, 27, 30, 34, 81, 82, 85, 86, 88, 131, 133, 136, 137, 139, 145–147, 150, 151, 153, 158

M

Mastery, 8, 22, 33, 40, 52, 70–72, 86, 87, 100–103, 110, 121
Matthew effects, 33, 36, 39
Metacognition, 62
Miller, G., 141
Multiple-choice, 48, 56, 68, 70
Myopia, 162

N

National achievement test, 3, 4
National curriculum, 4, 15
National standards, 13
New math, 13
Norm-referenced assessment, 10, 22, 44–48, 50, 51, 57, 102, 105, 109–111, 122, 125, 127, 152
Norms, 6, 11, 12, 17, 47, 48

O

Off-task behavior, 21, 42, 89
On-task time, 42

P

Pany, O., 47
Performance-based assessment, 45, 56–59, 87, 127
Powell, L., 153
Practice, 33, 37, 38
Problem-solving, 14, 78, 88
Proficiency tests, 8, 9
Prompts, 100, 101

R

Raw scores, 48
Readiness, 80, 81, 85, 143, 144, 146
Readiness tests, 44, 49, 50
Reed, M., 33, 72
Reliability, 58–60, 64–72, 79, 80
Repetition, 37, 38
Retention, 19

S

Salvia, J., 5, 47
Self-assessment, 91, 92
Self-esteem, 27, 28, 128
Shinn, M., 53
Simon, H., 41
Smiley, F., 157
Social utility, 13
Spache, G., 143
Specialists, 93–96, 138, 148–151
Snellen test, 161
Standard error of measurement, 69
Standard scores, 47, 49
Standardized tests, 5, 6, 9, 10, 24, 49, 50, 68, 70, 74, 77, 83, 85, 124
Stanovich, K., 33
Starch, D., 58, 67, 68
Subscription schools, 15, 16
Substantive assessment, 22, 24, 45, 126, 127
Success, 25, 27, 32, 33–37, 41–44, 59, 80, 89, 90, 97, 128, 155
Success-based assessment, 24, 36, 128, 141, 154, 156
Summative testing, 54, 56

T

Task analysis, 52, 53
Terhaar-Yonkers, M., 29, 33, 72
Tolerance limits, 142, 143, 146
Topping, K., 157
True/false, 68, 70
Tucker, J., 53, 71, 73

V

Validity, 4, 5, 64, 72, 75, 94, 95, 97–99
Validity, concurrent, 76
Validity, content, 7–9, 11, 12, 15, 22, 23, 47–50, 52, 54, 66, 73, 74, 76, 77, 79
Validity, construct, 62, 63, 77, 78
Validity, criterion-related, 75, 76
Validity, predictive, 49, 76, 77
Vision testing, 160–164
Visual acuity, 161

W

Whole language, 14
Williams, P., 33, 72
Wittrock, D., 33, 72
Word calling, 31
Written composition, 32